A TASTE
OF LEEDS

A TASTE OF LEEDS

PETER BREARS

Breedon Books
Publishing Company
Derby

First published in Great Britain by
The Breedon Books Publishing Company Limited
Breedon House, 44 Friar Gate, Derby, DE1 1DA.
1998

Front cover shows a selection of traditional Twelfth Night food
from Leeds including a Yorkshire Christmas Pie, a bowl of
Lambswool, a Twelfth Cake, eaten with cheese, and a tall
moulded Tipsy Cake. Back cover shows packing up a lunch
with soft oatcakes and oven-bottom cakes in the 1850s

ISBN 1 85983 140 0

Printed and finished by Butler & Tanner Ltd., Selwood Printing Works,
Caxton Road, Frome, Somerset.

Colour separations by Freelance Repro, Leicester.

Jackets printed by Lawrence-Allen, Avon.

CONTENTS

INTRODUCTION

FOOD is a fascinating subject, being far more than a means of sustaining life. To some, its major function is to promote good health, to others its purpose is to give superb sensory pleasure, while some companies treat it as an important trading commodity, a means of generating profit. Here, in this book, it is considered in yet another way, as one of the major elements in our changing way of life. Back in 1825, Brillat Savarin, the great French gastronome, had claimed, "Tell me what you eat: I will tell you what you are," recognising that the quality, quantity and composition of a person's food was one of the clearest indicators of their national, regional and social origins.

Here in Leeds, as in other parts of the world, the original diet eaten by most people was based on those foods which could be grown locally. The mainstays were cattle, sheep and pigs for meat, and oats for cereals, all these flourishing even on the acid soils and heavy clays of the local Pennine foothills. From at least a thousand years ago, when this area had a Scandinavian culture (which gave us all the local "-thorpe" and "-ley" placenames) the basic diet included such Scandinavian-style elements as oat crispbreads which died out only in the mid-19th century. During the 17th and 18th centuries, the merchants of Leeds began to adopt the countrywide middle-class diet, which included far more game, delicate fish, soft fruits, etc., along with sugar, spices, citrus and dried fruits, wines, etc., imported from overseas. The Industrial Revolution, which really began to affect Leeds from the early 19th century, brought with it both the most desperate poverty – with sub-subsistance working-class diets of bad bread and adulterated coffee at the bottom end of the scale – and the greatest wealth – wholesome,

plentiful meals and unbelievably sumptuous banquets for the business and professional classes – at the other. This was also the period in which Britain's great trading empire brought in new cheap supplies of fresh and dried fruits, various new cereals, canned and then frozen meats, etc., which enabled everyone to enjoy a much better, and much more varied diet, international in its origins, but very English in the ways in which it was prepared and eaten.

In the following pages we will look at each of these different lifestyles and their associated food traditions in some detail, drawing together all the available evidence contained in sources as diverse as diaries, dialect poetry, banqueting menus and local recipe books. The result is not only a fascinating record of how people lived, cooked and ate in Leeds in the Georgian, Victorian and Edwardian periods, but also a rich source of authentic period recipes, all of which have been rewritten so that they may be recreated in any modern kitchen.

It has long been assumed that all the best food in England comes from the countryside. You have only to look at the numerous "Country…" magazines in the newsagents, the various "Farmhouse…" cookery books, or the country-style kitchens supplied by the leading modern designers to appreciate the popularity of this view. However, the countryside has never had a monopoly of fine food, some of the meals served in great cities such as Leeds being as good as any served anywhere in the world. To date very little has been written on Britain's urban cookery traditions, but, as will be seen here, it is an amazingly diverse and interesting subject, one which combines the appeal of local history and practical cookery to present a revealing view of the past.

BRINGING IN THE FOOD

ECONOMIC success always depends upon trade, and as every trader knows, there is one factor which is absolutely essential for continuing prosperity, a really good location. It is this feature which has always guaranteed Leeds' great success. For a thousand years or more, England's major north-south trade route has followed the line of least resistance, passing between the flat boggy lands and wide rivers to the east, and the steep Pennine hills to the west, proceeding by way of Derby, Sheffield, Wakefield and Leeds, the routes taken today by the A61 and the M1 motorway. For east-west trade, meanwhile, the Aire Gap provided the easiest crossing over the Pennines anywhere between Derbyshire and Scotland. Since Leeds lay on the precise crossroads of these major routes, it was the ideal place for people to come to exchange their goods and foster a thriving market. These advantages were probably recognised by the Romans, who built a camp on Quarry Hill, and the Anglo-Saxons, who established a royal estate here in the seventh century. It certainly was apparent to Maurice Paynel, the medieval lord of the manor, who in 1207 created the borough of Leeds, marking out Briggate and its adjoining properties at their present size to form one of the largest market-places in Europe.[1]

Five hundred years later, at the opening of the 18th century, the Tuesday and Saturday Briggate markets were still as successful as ever. At its foot, between Leeds Bridge and Boar Lane, the handloom weavers from the Pennine foothills brought in their completed pieces of woollen cloth to sell in the early mornings.[2] Their places were then taken by dealers in linens, footware, woodware, basketry and, most importantly, fruit, vast quantities of which were bought here for resale in the Halifax market some 15 miles inland, as many as 500 cartloads of apples being sold here in a single day. Above Boar Lane came market for milk-cows, followed by the fish market where the pannier-men brought in a great variety of fish which they had carried by packhorse from the North Yorkshire coast, by way of Malton, York and Tadcaster. Just by the junction with Commercial Street and Kirkgate, the centre of the Briggate market-place was occupied by the Moot Hall, its first-floor courthouse lying over rows of open-fronted butchers' shops known as the Shambles to one side, and wool dealers to the other. Beyond it stood the butter-cross, a long low-roofed building set on pillars, where poultry and dairy produce were sold, the final open stretch of Briggate leading up to the Headrow being occupied by a busy corn market. As Daniel Defoe stated, Leeds had the greatest provision market in the north of England.[3]

In 1757, the poet John Dyer saw supplies being carried here from the surrounding countryside.[4]

The creaking wain brings copious store of corn,
The grazier's sleeky kine obstruct the roads,
The neat-dress'd housewives, for the festal board,
Crown'd with full baskets, in the field-way paths,
Come tripping on…

Over the next 100 years this trade in fresh foods continued to expand, keeping pace with the rapid growth of the town as a major trading and manufacturing centre. Despite its great size, Briggate now became far too congested, even after the Moot Hall and Cross were demolished in 1825, and so an impressive series of new markets had to be built around the town centre. The cloth markets had already been removed into the Coloured Cloth Hall in City Square in 1758, and the White Cloth Halls of 1711, 1756 and 1776, but even greater changes came in the 1820s boom which followed the end of the Napoleonic wars. Now the fruit and vegetable market moved on to its present site in Vicar Lane in 1822, while other stalls moved to the South Market built to the south of Leeds Bridge in 1823. The Shambles and fish market moved on to the site of the Victoria Quarter in 1825, further stalls then opening in a new Central Market on Duncan Street in 1827, the same year that an elegant Corn Exchange opened on the site of New Briggate.[5]

The Leeds Shambles stood in the centre of Briggate, opposite the present Queen's Arcade. Slaughtering took place in the street here probably from the early 13th century through to 1825-6, when these buildings were demolished.

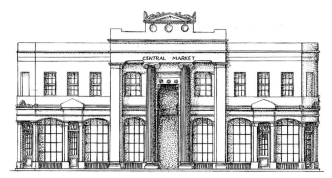

The Leeds Central Market, built at the junction of Duncan Street and New Market Street in 1824-7, was described as "one of the greatest ornaments to the town'. Its Grecian Ionic facade, with its elegant shopfronts, enclosed a spacious interior with three rows of shops, a gallery and a bazaar.

At this period quantities of food were still being grown locally. In the villages around Leeds, many people kept poultry, a pig or two, and cultivated their small garden plots, while manufacturers such as Benjamin Gott divided fields adjacent to their vast woollen mills into allotments where their workers could grow some of their own vegetables. Local farmers still raised arable crops of wheat, barley, oats, potatoes, greens, etc., as well as keeping cattle and sheep for meat, and herds of cows to provide the town with its milk, cream and butter. There were market gardeners, too, who specialised in the more delicate vegetables and fruits for the Leeds markets. For the herbs used both as flavourings and as home medicines, herb-gardens were set up. One at Mill Green in Holbeck sold 19 varieties which were made up into sixpenny (2.5p) bundles for sale early each morning to street traders who hawked them from door to door. Large quantities of peppermint and pennyroyal were also grown and distilled here, the peppermint oil being bought by humbug-makers in Holbeck, and some of the remaining peppermint water being sold to neighbouring mills to revive those girls who had been overcome by the heat. The roots of Solomon's Seal were in great demand on Sunday mornings, for men used them to cure the black eyes they had received in Saturday night fights.[6]

Since the earliest times the clear waters of the river Aire had also provided the people of Leeds with a source of food for the table, William Lodge's engraving of the town published in 1712 showing groups of men sitting with their rods and lines on the riverbank at Holbeck. The healthy state of the river was clearly illustrated by the many tons of dead fish which built up against Leeds Bridge after they were poisoned by the peaty waters from the great Ponden bog-burst upstream from Haworth in 1824.[7] Fish stocks soon recovered, so that both salmon and trout could once more be caught by fly-fishing at the foot of Kirkstall Abbey weir in the 1850s, while just downstream men in the Abbey Mill yard could catch dace and roach using maggots as bait. When the river was in flood, Mr Haywood caught fish at Armley using a net on a pole, then sold them around the village, a similar frame net being used by Mr Goodyear, Keeper at Kirkstall Clough, to take eels and other course fish for food.[8] Downstream from Leeds, fishing was such a popular activity that two public houses provided appropriate refreshments, the Fisherman's Arms being on Hunslet Lane, and the Fisherman's Hut across the river on Ellerby Lane, where it still operates today. By the 1860s, however, the increasing pollution caused by raw sewage, factory, dyeworks and chemical works effluent, and all manner of refuse from the riverside towns, finally killed off the fish population throughout the industrialised stretch of the river.

For much of its basic bulk foods, Georgian and early Victorian Leeds relied on its traditional sources of supply. A large proportion of its beef, for example, was herded down from Scotland into the Great Close pasture on Malham Moor from where, in the 1780s, 20,000 head of cattle could be sold each summer to drovers who brought them by six to 12 mile stages into the industrial West Riding market towns.[9] Many tons of oats for porridge and oatcake were imported from Holland, some of this being used as seed by the farmers of Ryedale, the

Here we see the sailing barges on the river at the Aire & Calder Navigation Docks around 1870. As Daniel Defoe described, about 1700 these vessels were bringing in butter, cheese, salt, sugar, fruit, spices, hops, oil, wine, brandy and other groceries for sale in the town, and then carrying away its cloth and coal down to the ports for export.

fertile area around Malton, Pickering and Helmsley in the North Riding. Once their crops had ripened in mid-August, they were in such great demand that they were not harvested into stacks or barns, but were actually threshed in the fields, the oat grain then being loaded into sailing barges at Malton, taken down the Derwent, along the Ouse, and up the Aire and Calder Navigation which had made the river navigable into Leeds in 1698. The navigation also enabled foods which had been imported from overseas, or from the specialist London suppliers, to be brought directly into the town by way of the port of Hull. Road transport was important for bringing in wagonloads of goods from London, York, and the surrounding countryside, the combination of new turnpike roads and fast mail coaches even enabling John Norton to start selling fresh oysters in Leeds in 1826.[10]

A few years earlier, in 1812, the Leeds engineer Matthew Murray had produced a new machine which would eventually revolutionise food supplies not only for Leeds, but for all the developed world. Working at his famous Round Foundry in Holbeck, he transformed the prototype steam locomotives, which were little better than mechanical curiosities, into very practical and economical carriers of heavy goods.[11] His 1812 engines, the world's first successful commercial steam locomotives, were used on the lines which carried coal from the Middleton Collieries down to the Hunslet coal staithes, but over the next 40 years more powerful locomotives had enabled a nationwide railway system to slowly emerge. By the 1870s Leeds was no longer dependent on slow-sailing barges and rumbling horse-drawn wagons for the delivery and despatch of its goods, for it was now at the heart of an efficient network, which brought it to within a few hours travel of the major ports.

In 1812 Matthew Murray built the world's first commercially successful steam locomotive to carry coal from the Middleton Collieries down to the coal staithes at Hunslet, as shown in George Walker's watercolour of 1814.

The use of steam power both for transport and for driving machinery made it possible for the town to thrive and expand as never before, thousands of people coming from all parts of England, Scotland and Ireland to take the new jobs being created here from the 1820s and '30s onwards. To meet the increasing demand for food, the railways brought in tons of grain and dry goods both from this country, and imported from the colonies and America. They also carried in fish from the ports, and, from the 1860s, tinned meats from Australia and Chicago, these being followed in the 1880s by refrigerated shiploads of frozen meat from Australia, New Zealand, North America and the Argentine.[12] Natural ice from America, Norway and Greenland were also brought in by rail to keep meat and fish really fresh, and for making ice creams.[13] Many people will still remember the large stone polar bear which peered down into New York Street from the front of the

Yorkshire Pure Ice Company's warehouse, from where natural ice, and later machine-made ice, was supplied to the Leeds butchers, fishmongers and confectioners.

The railway also proved invaluable for moving cattle, and its trucks gradually absorbed the herds which had formerly been driven down the hot, dusty roads. In 1855 the Corporation removed the cattle market from the open streets into the new Smithfield Cattle Market on North Street, but this was replaced in 1868 by the 16-acre Victoria Cattle Market on Geldard Road. Although this was a great improvement, the slaughterhouses remained in an appalling condition in the centre of town, where all their gross sights, smells and noises were obvious to all who walked along upper Briggate or Vicar Lane. Only in 1898-99 was a new Wholesale Meat Market and Abbatoir erected on New York Street, directly behind the City Markets. It was one of the finest facilities of its kind, being featured in the leading textbooks of the day, and successfully providing the city with good meat for the next 60 years.[14] For the sale of fruit, vegetables and general goods, the Corporation then completed its rebuilding of the City Markets on Vicar Lane in 1903-04. With its magnificent Renaissance frontage and huge iron-framed hall, it remains the most impressive market building in the whole of Britain.

A rather unexpected aspect of the railway is the effect it had on the local agricultural scene. Back in the early 17th century, Sir Matthew Lister, physician to King Charles I, had first brought the seeds of English or garden rhubarb, *Rheum rhaponticum*, into England, where John Parkinson, the King's Herbalist, grew specimens in his London gardens. By the 1790s it was to be found in many kitchen gardens, the coarse sharp-tasting green stalks being cut into small sections and cooked in pies, as a substitute for gooseberries. In 1824, a Scottish gardener called James Smith had discovered that by keeping the roots in the dark, they sent out fine, thin red stalks with a far superior colour,

The Leadenhall slaughterhouse stood in Vicar Lane, near the present Victoria Street arcade, up to the 1890s, bringing all its noise, squalor and stench into the heart of the main shopping and commercial centre. This is one instance where we should be grateful that colour photography was still a thing of the future. (*Leeds Library & Information Services*).

texture and flavour. This technique was then developed on a commercial scale in the "Rhubarb Triangle" between Leeds, Wakefield and Morley, where the climate, the plentiful fertilising waste from the towns, the cheap coal, and the railways, were ideal for its production. By the 1870s the roots were being dug out of the fields near Kirkstall Bridge, in Hunslet, etc., and placed in long, low and perfectly dark heated sheds between November and February. After a month or six weeks, the buds burst and the forced rhubarb stalks quickly emerged, these then being hand-picked by candlelight ready to be sold for use as a fruit from early December, when other native fruits were at their most expensive.[15] On 9 December 1904, one writer noted: "Leeds is famous, it might be said throughout Europe, for its early rhubarb, and already the first pale stalks of the luscious comestible have made their appearance on the market… Several London agents have already been in the city, while even agents from Paris are also on the scene."[16]

By this time the despatch of rhubarb to London by rail was already a well-established practice, the Great Northern's "Rhubarb Train" leaving Leeds every evening with between 60 and 160 tons of rhubarb ready for sale at the Covent Garden wholesale market early next morning. Rhubarb was also greatly enjoyed locally, where, known as "tusky", it was made into everything from the simplest stewed rhubarb and custard, to the finest of jams, chutneys, and an amazing range of desserts, sauces and wines.

By enabling foodstuffs, fuel and containers such as glass bottles, pottery jars and tins to be cheaply and quickly moved from one place to another around the country, the railways enabled food to be prepared and packaged on a completely new industrial scale. Now, as Britain ceased to be predominantly rural, and transformed itself into the world's first great industrial nation, there were ever-greater demands for quickly-prepared convenience foods. Instead of grinding their own mustard, preparing their own gelatin from calves' feet, and making their meals only from basic raw ingredients, all levels of society now wanted to save time and money by buying much of their food ready-processed. The thousands of women who now had to combine full-time jobs in the mills with their traditional roles as mothers and housekeepers had far less time to spend on domestic activities, for example, and really did need tasty foods which could be quickly cooked and served. Soon great manufacturing cities such as Leeds set about industrialising many aspects of the food trade, various companies developing and marketing a wide range of products for sale locally, nationally, and for export. Here are details of just a few of them.

In 1863, for example, Mr R. Goodall set up his business in Leeds, being joined in 1865 by Messrs Backhouse and Powell, to form the well-known company of Goodall & Backhouse, manufacturing grocers. Their White Horse Street premises occupied 70,000 sq ft of buildings to the south of Boar Lane, with a further 108,000 sq ft of factories between Sovereign Street and the river. Here their staff of 500 produced thousands of packets of egg powders, custard powders, blancmange powders, baking powders, jelly squares, quinine wine and ginger beer powders, as well as the tins in which many of them were sold. Their most important product, however, was "Yorkshire Relish", a commercially manufactured version of the black treacle, vinegar and spice mixture traditionally known in the county as "Yorkshire Dip", or "Yorkshire Ploughman's Salad". It bore a resemblance to Worcestershire Sauce, but was

THE ILLUSTRATED LONDON NEWS, Sept. 24, 1898.– 461

"THE KING OF THE CRUET."

YORKSHIRE — RELISH

The Most Delicious Sauce in the World.
Makes the Plainest Viands Palatable and the Daintiest Dishes more Delicious.
Enriches Soups, Stews, Chops, Steaks, Fish, &c.
Sold in Bottles, 6d., 1s., and 2s. each, of all Grocers, Stores, &c.
BEWARE OF SUBSTITUTES.

Sole Proprietors : GOODALL, BACKHOUSE & CO., LEEDS.

Selling over six million bottles a year, *Yorkshire Relish* was the world's most popular sauce. Although it was used in good-quality cookery, its main benefit was to give flavour and piquancy to many basic everyday meals.

far more popular, selling over six million bottles every year, the best-selling sauce in the entire world. Resplendent in its printed label, complete with its blue willow-pattern trade-mark, it featured in a wealth of dramatic advertising posters, for much of Goodall & Backhouse's success was due to their pioneering marketing techniques.[17]

In 1876 they published one of the earliest, and certainly most popular and successful of all Victorian promotional cookery books. Entitled *Good Things Made, Said and Done*, it had run through 42 editions before 1914. Each copy contains a selection of recipes for soups, fish, meat, biscuits, cakes, etc., which all include at least one of their products. In addition, there is a wealth of practical advice, such as:

TINNED MEATS

In the present day, when fresh butcher's meat has reached a price which makes Materfamilias sigh and Paterfamilias do a little more than sigh …attention should be given to the tinned meats from Australia and America …Tinned meats, that from Chicago excepted, have the appearance of being overdone …but the worst point about them is that they are somewhat insipid. This, however, can quickly and easily remedied by the addition of some YORKSHIRE RELISH.

In addition a series of four mottoes and homilies were set in a border around each page, typical examples including:

Diet cures more than physic.

Eat not to dullness.

Unquiet meals make ill digestion, etc.

BAKED TOMATOES.

MATERIALS.—Eight or ten tomatoes ; a thick slice of bread, well crumbled ; two ounces of butter ; pepper and salt to taste.

THE TOMATO.

PROCESS.—Scald the tomatoes with boiling water, cut them in thick slices without removing the stem ; rub the sides of a pie-dish with butter, or a little lard or dripping which will do as well, and lay in the slices of tomato ; season well with pepper and salt ; cover with bread crumbs, and scatter some small lumps of butter over the crumbs. Bake in a hot oven for from twenty to thirty minutes.

☞ *This dish may be considerably improved by pouring over the tomatoes, before adding the crumbs and butter, two or three tablespoonfuls of* YORKSHIRE RELISH, *the piquant sauce manufactured by Messrs. Goodall, Backhouse, and Co., of Leeds, and sold by all grocers and oilmen.*

With what should tomatoes be eaten?
Any meat, hot or cold. They are delicious either cooked or raw. When eaten raw they should be cut in slices and dressed as cucumber, some onion being added, chopped fine or cut in slices. Tomatoes should be eaten freely by all persons who are dyspeptic, or who suffer from torpid liver, on account of their valuable medicinal properties.
Are not tomatoes expensive?
English-grown tomatoes are, generally speaking, dear, as much as 8*d.* per pound being often asked for them. The cheapest are those which are sent to us from America in tins.

Goodall and Backhouse were one of Britain's leading producers of bottled sauces and packet foods. Their great success was built on very efficient advertising campaigns, which included the pioneering promotional cookery book *Good Things Made, Said and Done*, issued regularly from 1876. Here is a sample page, surrounded by its characteristic mottoes.

On a smaller scale, R. S. Brownhill & Sons of Savile Street, off Wellington Street, set up as confectioners around 1860, and then went on to produce "Feculina", a series of instant cake mixes for making snow, coconut, sponge and rice cakes.[18]

A number of fruit, jam and marmalade manufacturers also set up in Leeds about this time, most of them buying in their soft fruits from the English growers or from the wholesale merchants. They included Thomas Sunderland of Wortley Lane, William Moorhouse of Lofthouse Place, Holgates of Geldard Road, and John Hudson of Whitehall Road, who, founded around 1863, actually grew all the gooseberries, raspberries and strawberries used in his jams. Meanwhile in Bramley, Septimus Smith's factory, commenced in 1889, despatched some 20,000 packs of jam and marmalade every week, a clear indication of the scale of this virtually forgotten Leeds industry.

Other major processors included Brooke, Bond & Co, wholesale tea blenders. Founded in 1870, their Yorkshire Tea Warehouse at 11 Boar Lane was the centre of a nationwide distribution system which employed some 800 agents throughout the country.[19] These industries all depended on materials which were brought into Leeds from very con-

siderable distances, but there were others which grew out of locally available materials and skills.

Throughout the 19th century, Leeds was a major centre for the manufacture of mustard. The actual crop was mainly grown in the flat, fertile fields around York, where it was sown in early May and harvested in September, when the seeds were threshed out by the farmer ready for sale to the seed crushers and mustard manufacturers. Most of the Leeds mills which undertook this type of work crushed and ground a great variety of other materials, including spices, corn, peas and beans, dyewoods for the textile industry, oak bark for the tanneries, flint for the potteries, linseed and rapeseed for oils, and chalk and other minerals for making paints. Among those who concentrated on the mustard trade, the most important was J. & J. Armistead of the Water Hall Mills in Water Lane, who were in operation from 1748 through to around 1880. By selecting the finest seed and preparing it "by a peculiar process, ensuring its full strength and flavour" their product was claimed to be

J. & J. ARMISTEAD,

SEED CRUSHERS

AND OIL MERCHANTS,

MUSTARD & BRUSH MANUFACTURERS,

WATER HALL MILLS,

WATER-LANE, LEEDS;

AND

148½, FENCHURCH STREET,

LONDON.

ARMISTEAD'S MUSTARD

Has obtained a deserved celebrity, for its excellent quality. Being prepared by a peculiar process, the full strength and flavour of the seed are preserved, and it is decidedly

THE BEST FOR FAMILY USE,

FOR MEDICAL PURPOSES,

OR FOR EXPORT.

3 E   49

Leeds was a major mustard-grinding centre from the 18th century, its leading firm being J. & J. Armistead of Water Hall Mills, Holbeck.

the most economical for family use, the best for medical purposes such as plasters and baths, and particularly suitable for export, keeping well in all climates. Other manufacturers included Jonathan Lupton of Oil Mill Lane in the 1820s and William Thurman and Henry Thorne of Nevile Street from the 1840s, the latter's "Genuine" and "Double Superfine" brands being "highly recommended for family use". In 1862 the "'goodness, purity and quality" of the Durham Mustard made by R. & J. Harrison of Jack Lane Mills won them the sole prize in this section at the International Exhibition in London, "Durham" being the general name given to the mustards originally made in that city, but then continued in Leeds and York. By the 1890s, however, the Leeds mustard industry had gone into a terminal decline, only Henry Thorne continuing in this trade. Undoubtedly this was due to the arrival of J. & J. Colman of Norwich, who had set up at 46 Boar Lane as part of their rapid expansion throughout Britain and its colonies.[20]

Just as the Leeds grinding mills had fostered the mustard industry, the town's leather industry, the greatest in the country, promoted the manufacture of gelatin. By the 1890s, Richard Thackray was making gelatin at Newlay, but all the other producers, Astley, Cooper & Co, Samuel Greenwood and William Oldroyd, were all based in the leather-producing area of Meanwood Road, around Sackville Street, Proctor's Place and Scott Hall Street. Presumably they obtained all the skin, horns and hooves they required from the local tanneries, then boiled them down and clarified them both for industrial use and for human consumption. Oldroyds Scott Hall Mills made "Finest Powdered Calf Gelatin, Quality Unequalled", and published their own promotional recipe book to increase its sales.[21]

Back in 1812, when Matthew Murray made steam locomotion a practical means of transport, he can have had little appreciation of how his work would transform the economic and domestic lives of future generations. It is to the City's great shame that he has no statue in City Square, along with other Leeds worthies, especially when James Watt, the great Birmingham engineer, stands proudly among them. In Leeds terms, this man is particularly despicable, being so jealous and afraid of Murray's talents, that he bought up the land around the Round Foundry to prevent its expansion, employed its staff as industrial spies, secretly searched its workmen's luggage, and even attempted to set up an observation post in property overlooking the foundry yard.[22] These underhand activities brought him little success, however, for even by the 1830s his company had only supplied 15 per cent of the steam engines which powered local factories, all the others being constructed by Leeds engineers.

Notes

1. For a general history of Leeds see S. Burt & K. Grady, *The Illustrated History of Leeds*, Derby (1994)

2. R. Thoresby, *Ducatus Leodiensis*, (1715) 14

3. quoted in A. Heap & P. Brears, *Leeds Describ'd*, Derby (1993) 17

4. J. Dyer, *The Fleece*, (1775) in S. Johnson, *Works of the English Poets*, (1792) 92

5. Burt & Grady, *op.cit.*, 99

6. Yorkshire Archaeological Society MS 745

7. W. Turner, *A Springtime Saunter*, Halifax (1913) 176

8. Leeds Local History Library, *Local Notes & Queries* nos 431, 432, 704, 705, 774 & 775

9. G. N. Wright, *Roads & Trackways of the Yorkshire Dales*, Ashbourne (1985) 141

10. Anon., *The Industries of Yorkshire*, (1888) 62

11. E. K. Scott, *Matthew Murray, Pioneer Engineer*, Leeds (1928) 36, 38 et seq.

12. J. Burnett, *Plenty & Want*, (1966) 101

13. E. David, *Harvest of the Cold Months*, (1994) 326-8, 335-8, 343-7, 366-9, etc.

14. W. Douglas, *Douglas's Encyclopaedia*, 3rd ed. (n.d. c.1900) 2-10

15. See R. Giles *Forced Rhubarb in the West Riding of Yorkshire* (typescript 1970) Leeds Local History Library 338.17548/G39Y & *Leeds Mercury* 3/4/1905

16. *Yorkshire Evening Post* 9/12/1904

17. Anon., *Industries of Yorkshire*, (1888) 67, *A Century's Progress* (1893) 158 & E. Driver, *A Bibliography of Cookery Books Published in Britain 1875-1914*, (1989) 20-21 & 291

18. *Industries of Yorkshire, op.cit.*, 58

19. *Industries of Yorkshire, op.cit.*, 78

20. Leeds Local History Library, Bibliography 130, File on the Leeds Mustard Industry

21. *Kelly's Directory of Leeds*, (1897) & (1901), & Anon., *Quality Prepared Jelly Dishes with Oldroyd's Finest Powdered Calf Gelatin*, Leeds (n.d.)

22. Scott, *op.cit.*

HANDLOOM WEAVERS' PLAIN LIVING

DURING the 18th century, the West Riding's prosperous textile industry went through a period of massive expansion, its production increasing eight-fold, until it achieved almost two-thirds of the national output of woollen cloth.[1] In Leeds and its surrounding villages many working people were involved in the spinning, weaving, dyeing and finishing of coloured cloths, most of them working in small family units living in the local stone-built weavers' cottages. Following the traditional routine, the weaver would return from the Leeds cloth markets carrying the raw wool bought from one of the wool dealers beneath the Moot Hall, his womenfolk then perhaps washing or scouring it, carding it to make it light and fluffy, and then spinning it into yarn in the kitchen on the ground floor. He would then transform the yarn into a long warp, fit it into his loom upstairs, weave it into a complete piece of cloth, take it to be thickened and felted at a local fulling mill, dry it, and neatly fold it ready to be carried into Leeds for the next cloth market. There he would sell it to one of the Leeds merchants, using the money received to purchase provisions for his family, and more wool with which to repeat the process.

Some of the weavers' cottages had gardens where vegetables could be grown, or a pig could be kept, but since the domestic textile industry was an extremely time-consuming business, much of the food appears to have been bought in. Since Leeds lay in the Pennine foothills, its food was essentially that of upland Britain, where sheep, cattle, oats and some wheat represented the main produce. The diaries kept by Joseph Rogerson of Belle Isle Mill, Bramley, provide a useful account of the local farming year in the late Georgian period.[2]

In autumn and spring, the fields were prepared by ploughing and manuring with dung from the cattle-sheds, "willy-dust", the dry waste extracted from the first mechanical cleaning of the wool, and "seak", the wet sludge left after washing it. These were then "dreized" into the soil by having a

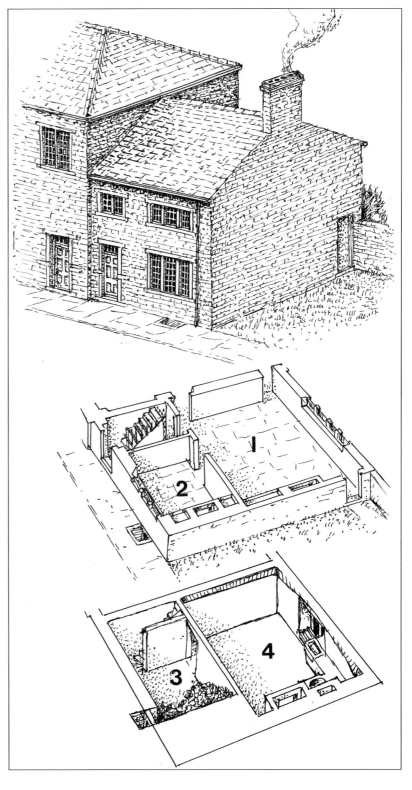

Most weaver's cottages around Leeds have either been demolished or considerably altered, but we can gain a good impression of their designs and accommodation from this block built at Armley Mills to the designs of John Sutcliffe of Halifax around 1793. It has large mullioned windows and stone-flagged ground floors to provide light and wet-working areas for the textile processes, while its first floor was open to the roof to make a large and airy loomshop.
Ground Floor
1. Kitchen/living room with cooking fireplace and cupboard
2. Parlour with fireplace and cupboards

Cellar
3. Coal cellar
4. Scullery with cooking fireplace, set-pot boiler and sink

harrow made of bushes dragged across the fields. Wheat was sown between October and January, and oats in March and April, these both being harvested between August and October, although everything depended on the weather. In September 1809, for example, the corn was "in a shocking condition, sadly sprouted, we have not got a sheaf yet …The stormiest Night for Wind and Rain I have seen this long time: it has scarce left a haddock [stook] standing in the fields: there cannot be worse weather".

As for the cattle, the milk-cows appear to have been wintered under cover from October through to February, when they were turned out into the fields during the daytime, only being kept out permanently from May or even June. Oxen for providing salt-beef for the winter months were bought at either the Leeds or Bradford fairs early in November, Joseph Rogerson recording:

Nov 10, 1808   Killing two oxen in our Cloth Mill.

Nov 12, 1808   The Oxen bought at Bradford stands to 7/- [35p] Pr. stone: we bought a hind Quarter for 6/3 [31p] Pr. Stone.

Nov 6, 1813   Recd. 2 Oxen from Grimthorpe.

Nov 15, 1813   Killing the two Oxen of Mr Marshall's.

As for the actual meals eaten by the weavers and their families, the first was breakfast, eaten just before 8 o'clock in the morning. By now they were ready for a meal, for they had already been woken by the blast of a horn at 5am, and had completed three hours work. In his mid-18th century poem *Matters of Interest in the Town of Leeds*,[3] Griffith Wright describes how:

'Ere clock strikes eight their called to breakfast,
And bowls of milk are brought in great haste,
Good Water-Pudding as heart could wish,
With spoons stuck round an earthen dish.

In other words, their breakfast was porridge.

Porridge

50 g/2oz medium or pin-head oatmeal
575ml/1pt water   5ml/1tsp salt
1. Bring the water to the boil, add the salt, and then sprinkle in the oatmeal with one hand while stirring with a spoon held in the other.
2. Continue stirring until the porridge is quite thick, then reduce to a very low heat and continue cooking, stirring occasionally for about 20-25 minutes, adding a little more water if it becomes too thick.

Traditionally in this area the single dish of porridge was placed in the centre of a round wooden table, all the family standing or sitting around, each taking spoonfuls from the communal dish, just as messes of pottage were eaten in noble households of the medieval period. Each person then dipped their spoonful of porridge into their personal bowl of milk, to cool it and moisten it before it was eaten. After breakfast all returned to work until midday when:

With wooden platter, bowl and ladle,
All seated round a scowered table,
Hard oaten cakes, some two or three,
In pieces fly, with fist and knee,
Tho' hard it in an instant doth.
Eat like soft manchet [bread] in the broth
Ere Tom or Jack have supped their mess,

With quick large strides comes 'prentice Bess,
Who, on earthen dish, with leg of mutton,
As good as knife was ever put in,
Each cuts a lunch [hunk], none care to inch it,
"First come-first serv'd" – They never flinch it!
But cram like Capons, while they eat!
All rise well pleased with their cheer,
Then march to spicket-pot for beer.
When quench'd their thirst, they quickly go,
And thro' the web the shuttle throw,
Thus they keep time with hand and feet
From five at morn till eight at *neet!*

The oatmeal used to make both the porridge and the oatcakes described here was one of the mainstays of the weaver's diet. Since the new oats made the finest oatcakes, they commanded the highest price, the *Leeds Mercury* of August 1800 announcing: "New Oats were sold in our market on Tuesday last [Aug 12th] when prices ranged from 3/9 [19p] to 6/3 [31p] a bushell.

Before being used the oats had to be carefully dried and then ground into meal. In 1788, when Thomas Lloyd was rebuilding Armley Mills as a centre where local weavers could come to have their wool mechanically carded ready for spinning, and their woven cloth fulled ready for sale, he included a purpose-built oatmeal plant, so that they could buy their oatmeal here at the same time.[4] The building, which survives today, had its own wharf on the banks of the Leeds and Liverpool Canal. From here one chute delivered coal down to the furnaces beneath a kiln, a heated masonry platform measuring 18 by 16ft (5.5 x 4.9 metres). A second chute delivered the oats on to the kiln, where they were gently turned to ensure that their flavour was never spoiled by being scorched or "fire-fanged" as they dried. Next the oats were shot down a wooden spout into the adjacent corn mill where a waterwheel powered two pairs of shelling stones, which removed the husks, two pairs of grey gritstones, which ground the oats into meal, and the boulting machine which graded it into fine oatmeal for making oatcakes, or coarse, for porridge.

To make the usual variety of oatcake, a process which it is almost impossible to undertake in a modern kitchen, the fine oatmeal was stirred into a tub of water or buttermilk, after which either a sourdough method, or added yeast, caused it to ferment overnight. A ladle-full was then poured on to a diagonally-scored board called a "backbrade", which had been sprinkled with dry oats, and the whole "reeled" around to form a large, round puddle of liquid batter. This was then baked by being slid on to a stone hotplate called a "baxston", the resulting oatcake resembling a large, thin, soft pancake.[5] Very poor people in Leeds used a much simpler method to make a kind of oatcake called clapcake:[6]

Clapcake

450g/1lb fine oatmeal
275ml/½pt tepid water
1. Pour the water into a bowl and stir it while sprinkling in 100g/4oz of the oatmeal to form a soft dough.
2. Knuckle this mixture down into the bowl until it forms a level, compact mass, and allow it to rest for a few minutes.
3. Put a large tablespoonful [20ml] of the mixture on to a handful of oatmeal spread on a baking board and knead it into a flat round cake about four inches in diameter.

In his watercolour of 1814 George Walker of Leeds shows how the local soft oatcake was made. Here the maker has just taken a ladle-full of oatmeal batter from the earthenware pancheon and pored it on to a bed of dry oatmeal on her "bakebread", which she is "reeling" round to form a thin puddle. She will next slide this on to the hot "baxton" behind her, and, after it is baked, cool it off on the back of the chair, and then hang it up on the "creel" above the fireplace to dry off to perfect crispness.

4. Sprinkle more oatmeal on to the baking board, put the cake on this, with a further sprinkling of meal, and proceed to roll it out, turning it occasionally, until it has formed a large, very thin oatcake.

5. Heat a metal girdle on the stove, until a little flour thrown on it slowly browns, but does not smoke.

6. Slip a piece of card [traditionally a thin, square board with a handle extending to one side, called a baking-spittle] under the oatcake, and use it to slide the oatcake on to the girdle, where it can be left for a few minutes until it has cooked, but has not browned.

Baxtons were made from a special type of mudstone which was quarried at Delph near Saddleworth, from where the smaller examples, perhaps a foot (30cm) round or oval, were carried in panniers on the sides of donkeys to be hawked around the streets of Leeds, the men crying out, "Baxtons!" to attract attention.[7] These were supported over the fire on fork-legged iron frames called "briggs" whenever they were required for use. When some old houses were being demolished in the Calls many years ago, they were found to have had much larger built-in baxtons measuring about a yard long by two feet wide by an inch and a quarter in thickness [91 x 61 x 3.2 cm], heated by their own separate fireplace beneath.

Once baked, the oatcakes could be stored dry and crisp on a "creel", a rack hanging from the ceiling above the fireplace. In the public houses in West Ardsley customers could help themselves from the creel, either nibbling it as it was, or perhaps throwing it on top of the coals on a clear fire to toast before putting it into their beer, to warm, thicken and flavour it. Some innkeepers soaked the oatcake in the gravy which dripped from the meat roasting before the fire, then salting it and distributing it as a special treat.[8] In most households, however, the oatcake was either eaten in its plain state, or was used either to make brewis, or to thicken broths. For brewis, it was crushed, put into a mug or bowl, scalded with boiling water to make it swell, drained, peppered and salted, and finally soaked in gravy to be served as a most delicious morsel.[9]

Griffith Wright's poem describes the oatcake being broken

up and put into the broth, where it quickly swelled and softened, to give the hot liquid more body and substance. The broth itself was a by-product of cooking the leg of mutton, for most people preferred to boil their meat, rather than roast it, since this was a far more economical and far less troublesome method of cookery. The basic methods were given in J. E. Thomas's *Housewife's Guide*, published in Leeds in 1830:

To Boil Beef or Mutton
Fresh meat must be put in when the water boils …Allow a quarter of an hour to every pound of meat, let it weigh more or less. When your meat is put in, and the water boils, take care to skim it very clean, otherwise the scum will boil down, stick to your meat, and will make it look black.
To do this today take 1.75-2.25kilo/4-5lb leg of lamb
1. Place a large pan of water on the stove and heat it to a rapid boil.
2. Put in the leg of lamb, boil it fiercely for 3 to 4 minutes, then reduce the heat until the water is only just bubbling, skim off any scum, then cover it and continue to simmer it very gently for about 1 hour 15 minutes.
3. Lift out the meat on to a hot plate, and keep it warm, then season the broth with a little salt and pepper, and serve it with oatcakes.

For the winter months, the November-killed beef was salted for perhaps two or three weeks, then rolled, pressed and hung up in a wood-burning chimney to dry for a month, thus preserving it as "Dutch beef", which could be cut into joints and boiled whenever it was needed. The following recipe, based on those used in Georgian Leeds, still gives good results:[10]

Dutch Beef
2kg/4lb brisket of beef, trimmed
50g/2oz dark brown sugar (muscovado)
225g/8oz coarse sea salt
15g/½oz saltpetre
1. Place the meat in a deep dish, rub in the sugar for 10-15 minutes, and leave in a cold place overnight, then rub it again, and leave it a second night.
2. Rub in the salt and saltpetre, turning and rubbing the meat each day for another four days.
3. Rinse the meat, form it into a roll, tying it in place with tape.
4. Put the meat in a pan of cold water, slowly bring it to the boil, then reduce the heat to a very gentle simmer for a further 2 hours or 2 hours 30 minutes.
5. Drain the meat and either serve it hot, in which case prepared cabbage, carrots or similar vegetables may be put in with the meat 30 minutes before serving, or press the meat overnight, and serve cold with pickles.

In later days, the weavers roasted their beef before the fire for their dinners, as described by John Bramley, a weaver in the village of the same name:

Ther't meyt hung dahn afore t'fire to rooast,
Ther's t'puddin' on t'brandree afore it ta tooast,
Potatoes top o't' hob, they'll be don enif sooin,
But Ah think tha can weive a few more bobbins bi nooin.

It is easy to imagine that scene, with the joint hung from the mantlepiece, probably on a loop of string which kept it rotating before the glowing coals in the hob grate, and the potatoes, perhaps some from the boatloads delivered to Joseph Rogerson at the canal wharf at Kirkstall Bridge in October 1813, simmering in the pot alongside. As the meat cooked, all its juices would be dropping on to the Yorkshire pudding resting before the fire in its dripping-tin, for, like all early Yorkshire puddings, it was cooked beneath the meat, first on one side and then the other, to emerge much heavier and greasier than the later oven-baked versions:

Yorkshire Pudding

1 large or 2 small eggs	*275ml/½pt mixed milk & water*
100g/4oz flour	*25g/1oz dripping*

pinch of salt

1. *Mix the flour and salt in a basin, and make a hole in the centre, break in the eggs and gradually add the milk and water, beating continuously to produce a smooth batter.*
2. *Leave the batter to rest for at least 30 minutes.*
3. *Pre-heat the oven to 200°C, 400°F, gas mark 6, put in the dripping in a dripping pan, and heat it until smoking hot.*
4. *Pour in the batter and bake for 30 minutes until crisp and brown, then cut into squares and serve.*

Although it was usually simply served with gravy as a separate first course, a variety of further ingredients were often mixed into the batter, the most common ones being:

1. *100g/2oz currants, for serving with pork.*
2. *1 large onion, boiled and chopped, and 5ml/1tsp dried sage, served with mutton or pork.*
3. *1 or 2 sticks of forced rhubarb cut into small pieces, and served as a dessert accompanied by a sweet white sauce.*
4. *Alternatively a small onion, sliced and separated into rings, was scattered on top of the batter just after it had been poured into the tin.*

Plain Yorkshire puddings were also spread or sprinkled with any of the following:

5. *Treacle or Golden Syrup.*
6. *Raspberry jam.*
7. *Raspberry jam and malt vinegar.*
8. *Mint sauce.*
9. *Mint sauce salad, made by mixing a handful of mint, finely chopped, with a finely shredded lettuce and spring onions, all dressed with sugar and vinegar.*
10. *Yorkshire Ploughman's Salad, 15ml/1tbs black treacle mixed with 30ml/2tbs malt vinegar, and a pinch of black pepper.*

As an alternative, especially when pork was being served, there might be a seasoned pudding [see p.60].

In the afternoon, on special occasions, the weaver's wife might invite her friends round for tea, even though this was still a very expensive luxury:

And while the good man is away
The neighbour-wives all set a day
To meet, and drink a dish of tea! …
When they have sat and chat a while,
The kettle is brought in to boil,
The Tea-Table in order spread,
Rolls buttered, cold, and some toasted!
"Bohea or Green, – mixed or clear?
Which will you please – do pray draw near!"
So we will leave them at their ease
And to discourse in what they please.

On most working days, spinning and weaving continued from the midday dinner through to eight at night, when:

Then call'd down e'er the clock gives warning.

Of Broth that is on the fire a-warming.

for broth, probably re-heated from dinner, formed their regular supper. In some cottages a very substantial broth was made from sheep's heads. These were cleaned, chopped in two, and the brains, tongue and eyes removed, although some people claimed that the eyes were left in, so that the head "would see them through the week"! After soaking in brine for a few hours, the head was simmered for two hours with potatoes, vegetables, pearl barley or lentils, and perhaps dumplings. The brains were enclosed within a cloth bag and suspended in the water by means of a string tied on to the saucepan handle, so that they would cook without sticking to the bottom of the pan. When all was ready, they would either be mashed with a little vinegar to form a brain sauce to accompany the head, or be eaten on toast with cream, butter and herbs as a great delicacy. As for the tongue, this was simmered, cooled, and then sliced to make into sandwiches.

On Tuesdays and Saturdays, being cloth-market days, the weavers had to take their pieces of cloth into Leeds early in the morning, frequently rising before dawn, travelling long distances along the ill-made roads, often in harsh wet weather. They then waited inside the inns which stood in Lower Briggate, until the innkeepers had erected the stalls in rows down each side of the street, and the market bell rang about 7am. By this time they needed something substantial to satisfy their cold and hunger. For this purpose, the landlords offered the Brigg-Shott, this curious name coming from the Brigg, the medieval Leeds Bridge on which the market was first held, and "shot", the payment for ale, or a round of drinks.

This meal was first described by Celia Feinnes who visited Leeds in 1698:[11] "If one calls for a tankard of Ale which is always a groate [about 2p], you may have a slice of meate either hott or cold according to the tyme of day you call, or else butter and Cheese gratis into the bargaine: this was a General Custom in most parts of Yorkshire, but now they have almost changed it, and tho' they still retaine the greate price for the ale, yet make strangers pay for their meate. There is still a Custome on a Market day at Leedes at the sign of the bush just by the Bridge, anybody that will goe and call for one Tanckard of ale and a pint of wine and pay for these only shall be set to a table to Eate with 2 or 3 dishes of good meate and a dish of sweetmeats after."

Ralph Thoresby, the Leeds cloth-merchant antiquary, then complained: "The Brig-End-Shots have made a great noise among the vulgar, where the clothier may, together with his Pot of Ale, have a Noggin o' Pottage and a Trencher of either Boil'd or Roast-Beef for Two Pence."[12]

This was confirmed by Defoe:[13] "The Refreshment given the Clothiers by the Inn-keepers (being a Pot of ale, a Noggin of Pottage, and a Trencher of broil'd or roast Beef, for Two-pence) is called the Brigg-shott to this day."

As these descriptions have shown, most working people in Georgian Leeds usually had a good basic diet, with problems only arising in times of scarcity due to bad harvests, etc. In May 1757, the Revd Henry Crooke, curate of Hunslet related this story: "About 10 …was alarmed by an uncommon Bustle in the Town, and being apprehensive that the Mob was rising upon account of the Dearness of the Corn, I went out among Em, and prevailed upon several to return to their respective Homes, and returned to my study."[14] Similarly, in May 1800 the high price of provisions caused the local people, especially the colliers, to riot at the market, so that the magistrates had to call out Colonel Lloyd's Leeds Volunteers to stand guard, while in August 1812: "Something like a Mob of Old Women in Leeds Corn Market today owing to a person wanting £4 Pr. Load for Wheat [over double the normal price] and wd. Take no less, so that he outstood his Market, and was the last on the ground- they took his corn and spread it on the floor."[15] Some relief was provided by the Soup Kitchen set up by public subscription in 1800, which served 2,400 pints of beef and vegetable soup every day, but, when things got really bad, and people were forced into the Workhouse at the top of Lady Lane, they were relatively well-fed with their usual everyday foods, as may be seen in the following diet sheet for October 1726:[16]

	Breakfast	Dinner	Supper
Sun.	bread & beer	beef & broth	milk porridge
Mon.	beef broth	rice milk	milk porridge
Tues.	milk porridge	plum porridge	bread & beer
Wed.	bread & cheese	beef & broth	milk porridge
Thurs.	beef broth	potatoes	bread & cheese
Fri.	bread & beer	rice milk	milk porridge
Sat.	water porridge & treacle	pease porridge	bread & beer

For most people, however, the booming textile industry had produced a real increase in their standard of living, Gamaliel Lloyd, a prosperous Leeds cloth merchant, commenting in 1800 that weavers' wages were "nearly triple what they were 40 or 45 years ago, & they work 2 or 3 hours less than they did at that time, being now universally paid by the measure, & not by the day, which 45 years ago was for a common weaver only 9d or 10d [5p] a day from five in the morning till nine at night, deducting the necessary time for meals. At that time & for several years after, the Clothiers bought an Ox or a Cow at the Leeds November fair & salted it. This with Water Grewel, Onions, & Bacon & Eggs, Oatcakes & salt butter, formed the principal food of the People. They now eat fresh meat, vegetables, & a good deal of wheat bread. This advance of wages opens to new wants and new desires."[17]

As Joseph Rogerson put it: "What with men Drinking Punch & women Drinking Tea, we are to have no more work done in this part. We shall be in want of another Bonaparte to make them work!"[18]

He was, after all, an employer, and not one of the employees.

Notes:
1. For general background reading see H. Heaton, *The Yorkshire Woollen and Worsted Industries*, Oxford (1965) & Crump, W. B. (ed), "The Leeds Woollen Industry", *Thoresby Society*, Leeds (1931)
2. E. Hargrave & W. B. Crump, "The Diary of Joseph Rogerson, Scribbling Miller of Bramley, 1808-1814", *Thoresby Society*, XXXII, Leeds (1929) 98
3. quoted in A. Heap & P. Brears, *Leeds Describ'd*, Derby (1993) 20-21
4. P. Brears, *Thomas Lloyd of Armley Mills*, Wakefield (1988) 16-19
5. Anon., *Dialect of Leeds*, (1862) "bakbrade" & "baxton"
6. *ibid.,* 268
7. *ibid.,* 241
8. *ibid., 277,* & J. H. Wilkinson, *Leeds Dialect Glossary & Lore*, Leeds (1924) 192
9. *ibid.,* 258
10. E. Moxon, *English Housewifery Exemplified,* Leeds (*c.*1749) 87, & A. Peckham, *The Complete English Cook*, Leeds (1773) 39
11. C. Fiennes, quoted in Heap & Brears, *op.cit.,*16
12. R. Thoresby, *Ducatus Leodiensis* (1715) 17
13. D. Defoe, quoted in Heap & Brears, *op.cit.,*17
14. quoted in S. Burt & K. Grady, *The Illustrated History of Leeds*, Derby (1994) 81
15. Hargrave & Crump, *op.cit.*
16. quoted in P. Brears, "Bastille Soup & Skilly", in C.A.Wilson (ed), *Food for the Community,* Edinburgh (1993) 123
17. Lloyd family MS, quoted in P. Brears, *Traditional Food in Yorkshire*, Edinburgh (1987) 9
18. Hargrave & Crump, *op.cit.*, 27/4/1814

THE FEAST

"I WISH the devil had him who first invented feasts," continued Joseph Rogerson on 30 August 1809.[1] "Our slubbers have not given over feasting yet: they have done nothing these three days past: they are a set of clever fellows. I doubt I shall see some of them be glad to work when they cannot get any."

Like many other mill-owners, he thought that feasts were a great waste of time and money, besides being a source of considerable trouble in the neighbourhood. The workpeople, however, held exactly the opposite view. For them it was the greatest celebration of the entire year, except for Christmas. It was their great annual holiday, a time for fun, games, good food, and the re-union of family and friends.

In addition to the Leeds Summer Fair, held each July, the major feast was Leeds Old Fair, held every November in Briggate, and which attracted up to 100,000 visitors from throughout the county, many coming here to buy the beef they needed for the coming winter. John Russel recorded that on 8 November 1799: "The shops were shut up, as the fair was for cattle. The whole of Briggate was filled. It was dangerous to pass, and droves [of cattle] passing other streets filled the whole town with bustle. On 9 November was the Toy Fair. A few irregular stalls with cakes, etc., were all I saw, with clowns I could not understand. Young women and men offering themselves for service stood about, to be hired for the year …The young people look cheerful, the women rather pretty, with round faces, and of a good colour, but when I hear them speak, I feel surprised at the different selection and pronunciation of words."[2] A more vivid description by Mr Isaac appeared in the *Leeds Mercury* in November 1789:

> Heigho! Drovers, bulldogs, oxen,
> Butchers bragging, landlords coaxing,
> Rapping, roaring, thumping, pricking,
> Poor dumb beasts – for only kicking …
>
> Wagons, cartmen, drums a rattling,
> Prudes in limbo, coquettes prattling,
> Raree show of short and long men,
> Bears and wolves and weak and strong men …
>
> Pockets empty, bills unpaid, and
> Rogues at dead of night afraid, and
> Many a bargain – if you'd strike it
> This is Leeds Fair, how d'ye like it?'

By the 19th century, the Leeds Summer and November fairs offered a mass of colourful attractions, ranging from theatre booths with lurid tragedies or puppet shows, to menageries exhibiting all manner of wild beasts, and circuses featuring tattooed ladies, living skeletons, petrified men, hairless horses (shaved each morning!), talking fish, giants, dwarfs, and even a wild South Sea Savage (actually born on Quarry Hill, but blacked up with soot!). For refreshments, the "Original Pea Shop" or "Uncle Tom's Cabin Pea Shop" sold hot boiled peas flavoured with vinegar, salt and pepper. There were also fruit stalls and traders offering parkin pigs, brandysnap and spiced cakes.[3]

Parkin Pigs

225g/8oz plain flour	5ml/1tsp bicarbonate of soda
225g/8oz medium oatmeal	pinch of salt
225g/8oz treacle	50g/2oz brown sugar
50g/2oz butter	5ml/1tsp ground ginger
a few currants	

1. Melt the butter, treacle and sugar together, and stir in to the remainder of the ingredients to form a stiff dough.
2. Turn out on to a floured board, roll out thinly, cut into pig shapes, add the currant eyes, and bake on greased baking sheets at 180°C, 350°F, gas mark 4 for 10-15 minutes.

Brandy Snap

50g/2oz butter	5ml/1tsp ground ginger
100g/4oz golden syrup	100g/4oz sugar
100g/4oz flour	a few drops of lemon juice

1. Rub the butter into the flour, and stir in the sugar, ginger, lemon juice, and melted, but still cool, golden syrup.
2. Place 5ml teaspoonfuls of the mixture on greased baking sheets, spacing them about 15cm/6ins apart, and bake them at 180°C, 350°F, gas mark 4 for 8-10 minutes.
3. Remove the sheets from the oven, allow them to cool for 1-2 minutes, then loosen them with a knife and roll them round the lightly greased handles of wooden spoons.

Spiced Cakes for a Feast, 1830

225 g/8oz plain flour	5ml /1tsp carraway seeds
125 g/5oz butter	50 g/2oz currants
100 g/4oz sugar	60-70ml/4-5tbs milk

1. Rub the butter into the flour and sugar, mix in the currants and carraway seeds, and work in just sufficient milk to form a stiff dough.
2. Turn the dough out on to a floured board, and form it into cakes about 8 cm/3ins in diameter by 2 cm/¾in thickness, nipping the edges to form an ornamental border.
3. Bake at 180°C, 350°F, gas mark 4 for 35-40 minutes.

Other special feast-time foods included flat gingerbread figures shaped in shallow wooden moulds. These were probably made by specialist bakers such as Francis Duffield who made brandysnap and gingerbread at his St Peter's Square premises up to the time of his death in 1904.[4] Similar results can be obtained today by stamping the dough with ornamental butter-pats:

Roll Gingerbread, 1830

450g/1lb black treacle	50g/2oz butter
100g/4oz fine oatmeal	10ml/2tsp ground ginger
450g/1lb plain flour	10ml/2tsp carraway seeds
glaze: 1 egg	75ml/3floz water
12g/½oz butter	

1. Rub the butter into the dry ingredients, then work in the treacle to produce a stiff dough, and knead this thoroughly.
2. Roll out 5cm/¼in thick on a floured board, dust with ginger, press into the moulds, or cut out in rounds, trim the edges, and place on greased baking sheets.

Around Leeds each local community arranged its own feast, its date perhaps coinciding with the saint's day of the parish church, while avoiding the feasts of neighbouring villages. At these events, the main streets were filled with rows of stalls, those set up at Pudsey in the 1820s selling dolls for the girls, and model horses, drums, trumpets, whips, etc., for the boys. There were also automata, Punch and Judy shows, swing boats, whirligigs, fat men, fat pigs, aunt sallies, peep-shows, circuses, and gambling tables for cards and dice. The feasts were the scene of athletic events too, Holbeck feast being famous for horse races, cock-fights, man fights, wrestling, and running.[5] At Bramley, meanwhile:[6]

> The morning comes, the feast begins, bazaars with toys are
> spread,
> The stalls are heaped with brandysnap, and nuts and
> gingerbread.
> The flyboats sail into the air, and drums and trumpets
> sound,
> While round about, with shriek and shout, the whirly-gigs
> go round.

In the home, preparations for the feast started the previous week, when all the walls were freshly whitewashed, the floors scoured, the furniture scrubbed and polished, and the metalwork all around the fireplace burnished to a high gloss.[7] Around Hunslet wives would exclaim, "Ah mun get cleeaned dahn for t'feeast," and go to their old druggist, Mr Wood, for their supplies of whitening to redecorate their rooms, since wallpaper had not yet come into fashion here. In fact, the week before the feast was actually known as "liver and whitewash" week, those who were saving up for their feast-time food feeding their families on two or threepennyworth of liver, fried up with onions. Great supplies of food and drink were then bought in, even if the family was very poor, for it was a matter of pride that on this day there should be no sign of poverty.

On the feast day itself, usually a Sunday when most friends and relatives were free to attend, all visitors to the village were free to call in and enjoy the hearty, open-handed hospitality, every house door standing permanently open for this purpose. For dinner, usually served at midday, the main dish was a great joint of roast beef, the largest and most impressive that the family could possibly afford. In the mid-19th century some Holbeck workmen earning only 24 shillings (£1.20) a week were buying massive joints of "Feast Beef" weighing up to 18lbs. This was hung down from the mantlepiece on a loop of string or from a clockwork bottle jack, so that it would roast evenly while rotating before the clear coal fire built up in the grate below. When it was done:

> But see how changed the joint of beef!
> The bones stand out in bold relief,

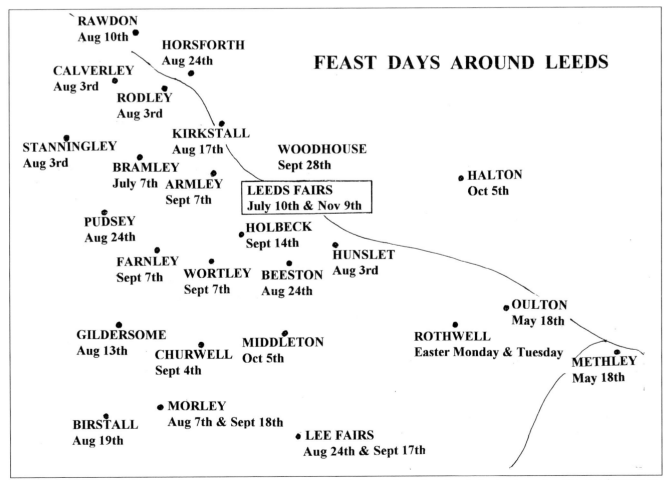

FEAST DAYS AROUND LEEDS

RAWDON
Aug 10th

HORSFORTH
Aug 24th

CALVERLEY
Aug 3rd

RODLEY
Aug 3rd

STANNINGLEY
Aug 3rd

KIRKSTALL
Aug 17th

WOODHOUSE
Sept 28th

BRAMLEY
July 7th

ARMLEY
Sept 7th

HALTON
Oct 5th

LEEDS FAIRS
July 10th & Nov 9th

PUDSEY
Aug 24th

HOLBECK
Sept 14th

HUNSLET
Aug 3rd

FARNLEY
Sept 7th

WORTLEY
Sept 7th

BEESTON
Aug 24th

OULTON
May 18th

GILDERSOME
Aug 13th

CHURWELL
Sept 4th

MIDDLETON
Oct 5th

ROTHWELL
Easter Monday & Tuesday

METHLEY
May 18th

MORLEY
Aug 7th & Sept 18th

BIRSTALL
Aug 19th

LEE FAIRS
Aug 24th & Sept 17th

Each village around Leeds held its feast in the summer months, most being in August and early September when the weather was at its best. Their dates were often published in local almanacs in the mid-19th century.

The meat shrinks in the shade:
Yet still how great are the supplies!
In fact the joint's so large a size,
It braves the knife's keen blade.

In addition to potatoes and boiled vegetables, the traditional accompaniments to the roast beef were:

Pickled Cabbage, 1733

1 red cabbage, about 900g/2lb	6 peppercorns
100g/4oz salt	25g/½oz root ginger
1,150ml/2pt malt vinegar	half nutmeg, cut in four

1. Quarter the cabbage vertically, remove the outer leaves and central stalk, then shred it finely.
2. Place the cabbage in a bowl, layering it with the salt, and leave overnight.
3. Rinse the cabbage in cold water, drain it, and pack it into jars.
4. Boil the spices in the vinegar for a minute, allow it to cool, pour it into the cabbage, seal it down, and use within the next few weeks.

Pickled Cucumber

1 cucumber	150ml/¼pint or less malt vinegar

Slice the cucumber thinly into a dish, cover with the vinegar, and use within the next two days.

Next a currant pudding usually appeared smoking hot, and if possible flamed with brandy, as the second course:

Plum Pudding, 1830

150g/6oz plain flour	300ml/½pt milk
150g/6oz raisins	1 egg, beaten
100g/4oz suet	50g/2oz sugar
pinch of salt	

1. Mix the dry ingredients in a bowl, make a well in the centre, and gradually beat in the egg and the milk, a little at a time, to produce a soft mixture.
2. Scald a piece of flannel or doubled muslin about 50cm/18ins square, sprinkle it with flour, gently shake off the surplus, and lay it across a basin.

Hunslet Feast was held around 3 August each year, just behind the old parish church of St Mary the Virgin, which was demolished in 1862. As this view shows, it featured all kinds of sweet and fruit stalls, swingboats, a roundabout, Punch and Judy show, and a showman's booth for performances.

3. Pack the mixture into the cloth, using the basin as a support, and tie the cloth tightly over the pudding, then lift it out of the basin and plunge it into a large pan of boiling water.
4. Cover the pan, and boil the pudding in it for 3 hours, topping it up with more boiling water as it evaporates.
5. When ready, lift the pudding from the pan, quickly plunge it into cold water, and turn it out on to a hot plate, and serve with a sweet white sauce.

Alternatively the pudding may be packed into a greased 850ml/1½pt basin, sealed with cooking foil, and steamed for 3 hours.

Pies formed the basis of the third course, a course of sweet desserts, as described in Richard Spencer's poem "Holbeck Feast": [8]

The snow-white cloth is neatly spread,
And graced with celery and bread,
With dishes, plates and glasses.
All is so very bright and clean,
The table's fit for any queen,
A credit to the lasses!
The kitchen table looks quite smart
O'erspread with many a tempting tart
And one enormous custard.
And other real, essential things
Such as befit the board of kings
As pepper, salt and mustard.
There is a host of goodly pies,
Besieged with swarms of busy flies
Some over them are creeping:
Some, as if wondering what is hid
Beneath the surface of the lid,
Are down the vent-hole peeping.

Fruit Pies

675g/1½lb fruit, such as apples (peeled, cored & sliced), plums (halved & the stones removed), gooseberries (topped & tailed), forced rhubarb (cut in 2.5cm/1in lengths)	
225g/8oz plain flour	100g/4oz lard
pinch of salt	45ml/3tbs (approx) cold water

1. For the pastry, rub the fat into the flour and salt, then use a round-bladed knife to work in the water, then knead lightly to form a smooth dough.
2. Roll out two-thirds of the pastry and use it to line a 20cm/8ins pie dish or flan tin, fill with the fruit layered with the sugar.
3. Roll out the remainder of the pastry to form a lid, dampen the edges of the pie, and press it in place, trim the edges, pierce a hole in the centre, and use the trimmings to make any decorations.
4. Brush the pastry with a little milk or water, dredge it with sugar, and bake at 220°C, 425°F, gas mark 7 for 15-20 minutes, then reduce the heat to 180°C, 350°F, gas mark 4 for a further 20-25 minutes.

After this great meal, its substantial fare probably washed down with strong home-brewed ale in most homes, both family and friends would rest for a while before setting off to spend the rest of the day amid the fun-fairs, theatricals and races on the

Cast in sugar-paste from carved wooden moulds, these miniature houses and the fronts of the Leeds Corn Exchange of 1828 (top) and the Commercial Buildings of 1826-9 (bottom), were probably sold at the Leeds Fair on Briggate.

example, the publicans to the east of the town centre mounted the "Quarry Hill and Famous City of Mab Races" in robust imitation of a grand race meeting. On the printed race list, the owners of the steeds, all local men, were graced with the titles of Duke, Earl, Lord, Sir, General, Colonel, Major or Captain, specially invented for this event, while the horses were given titles and pedigrees which were either entirely humorous, or referred to the public house they frequented, as in:

> Duke Hatf[ie]ld's bl. C. Bobbin, by Stuff, out of Shuttle.
> Lord Parf[i]t's br. F. Teazle, out of Golden Fleece, by Handle-setter.
> Lord Tiln[e]y's ro. C. Chisel, by Walling Stones, out of Square Compass.

After the sweepstakes, the Quarry Hill Stakes, the City of Mab Plate for half-bred Jack-Asses, the Burmantofts Town Plate, and the Top Close and Leylands Tradesmen's Stakes for half-bred horses, a grinning match was held at Quarry Hill, facetiously featuring "prominent Members of the Leeds Tee-Total Society who reside within the Preccincts of the Feast." Then, on the Wednesday, there was a bell race, sack race, greasy pole for a new hat, and a match at "brasses", a local game in which round pieces of iron or brass were pitched four or five yards, like quoits, with a copper kettle as a prize. For refreshment, "Old Hughey, the well-known Quarry-Hill Fruit Merchant, begs to inform his Friends that he has just returned from Hull, where he has purchased a Large Cargo of Real Barcelona Nuts, China Oranges, &c. And that he will feel great Pleasure in supplying the Company at the different Booths on the Race-Ground, when those who think proper may have a 'Go' at his Rolling Molly, *alias* Big Bess." This was probably some kind of fairground ride, "rolling molly" being the local word for a somersault.

Events of this kind clearly illustrate that the working-class inhabitants of Georgian and Victorian Leeds enjoyed a really rich and robust communal social life, even if they were frequently close to poverty. However hard life might be throughout the year, they used the institution of the feast to enjoy all the good things in life, with the best of food and drink, the best of good company, and the best communal entertainment being readily offered and partaken by all. The nature of the feast, and its place in local life, began to change around the 1880s, probably due to the increasing size of Leeds, which was perhaps becoming more impersonal as it grew from a provincial town into a great city. Certainly from this time the feast took on a much more commercial aspect, its centrepiece being the visiting fairground with its rides, shies and stalls, rather than the great meals for families and friends and the communally organised sports, which now went into a terminal decline.

feast-ground. Over the next couple of days visits would be paid to relatives or aquaintances, where cold roast beef and pickles would appear on the table, while any good customer at the local public house or shop would probably be invited to partake of further beef and pickles as a token of goodwill. On the Wednesday of feast week, all those who could afford it would set off for a day trip to some popular north country historic town or beauty spot. Here they enjoyed their last day of freedom and fun, relaxation and good living, for this was the end of their great summer holiday, and soon they would be back in the pits, factories and mills beneath the black skies and even blacker buildings of industrial Leeds.

From time to time, informal feast entertainments were organised by local innkeepers. On 29, 30 August 1836, for

---

Notes:

1. E. Hargrave & W. B. Crump, "The Diary of Joseph Rogerson of Bramley, Scribbling Miller, 1808-1814", *Thoresby Society* XXXII, Leeds (1929) 98

2. G. C. Williamson, *John Russel, R.A.*, (1894) 63

3. *Local Notes & Queries*, no.563-4 (1889): A. Mattison, "Memories from a Citizen at Leeds Summer Fair 60 Years Ago", *Yorkshire Evening Post*, 14/7/1937: *Yorkshire Observer*, 20/7/1912 & *Yorkshire Evening Post*, 13/7/1909

4. *Yorkshire Post*, 11/2/1904

5. *Leeds Mercury*, 12/9/1904

6. J. T. Barker, *The Pilgrimage of Memory*, (1885)

7. *Local Notes & Queries*, no.563, & *Yorkshire Evening Post* c.5/8/1905

8. R. Spencer, *Field Flowers*, Batley (1890) 52

FESTIVE FOODS

FOR thousands of years, good food has made special communal events both enjoyable and memorable, helping to draw families together and cement friendships. Some foods appear to have developed amazing long-term relationships with particular customs, the pig bones left in the graves of Yorkshiremen in the second century BC reminding us, for instance, of the funeral ham teas of our own times. This connection has often led to foods of the past surviving through to the present day. Frumenty, for example, a prehistoric whole-grain porridge, is still being made in Yorkshire on Christmas Eve, even though it has not been eaten at an ordinary everyday meal for centuries. In a similar way we still eat great roasts and rich steamed puddings on Christmas Day, long after these dishes have passed out of most normal diets. Fortunately, many details of local recipes and customs have survived from the past, so that we can now recreate the special traditional foods made and eaten here in Leeds over the last 200 years.

At the very start of life, the arrival of a new baby was usually celebrated by a party at the local pub, where the largely male company effectively "wetted the baby's head", although it was rarely present on these occasions. No particular food was connected with this event, except at Gomersal, where oval cakes or buns called "Dumb Boys" were served at the Old Black Bull on Garfitt Hill.[1] By the late 19th century, however, many families with middle-class aspirations were holding christening parties in their own homes, these being graced by special christening cakes bought from the confectioners.

At weddings, particularly in the surrounding villages, it was customary to start the day with all the men breakfasting at the groom's father's house, where rum posset was served before they collected their wives and lovers from a similar celebration at the bride's father's.[2] At the dinner served after the wedding, the major dish used to be the Bride Pie, which was crammed full of useful protein in the form of eggs, oysters, lamb's testicles, etc., to aid the physical needs of the newly-weds:[3]

To Make a Bride Pye, Ann Peckham, 1773

"*Parboil cock's combs, lamb-stones, and veal sweetbreads, blanch ox-palates, and cut them in slices: add to them a pint of oysters, slices of interlarded bacon, some blanched chestnuts, a handful of pine kernels, and some dates sliced: season them with salt, nutmeg and mace, and fill your pie with them: lay slices of butter over them, and close it up: when baked, take veal gravy, a handful of white wine, a little rolled butter rolled in flour, made hot, and pour in: so serve it up.*"

There was also a Bride Cake, the predecessor of the present wedding cake, a typical late Georgian example being given in J. E. Thomas's *New Whole Art of Confectionery* published in Leeds in 1830:[4]

Bride Cake

450g/1lb plain flour	8 eggs, separated
450g/1lb butter	450g /1lb currants
225g/8oz sugar	100g/4oz flaked almonds
¼tsp grated nutmeg	350g/12oz chopped mixed peel
¼tsp ground mace	75ml/3floz brandy

1. Line a 20cm/8ins round tin with greased greaseproof paper, and tie three layers of brown paper or newspaper around the outside to provide additional insulation.
2. Pre-heat the oven to 150°C, 300°F, gas mark 2.
3. Cream the butter with the sugar, mix in the egg whites, beaten to stiffness, and then the beaten egg yolks.
4. Fold in the flour, mace and nutmeg, then the brandy, almonds, and the dried fruits, etc.
5. Pour the mixture into the tin, and bake for about 3 hours 30 mins.

Very similar recipes were being baked in Leeds homes almost 50 years later, the following version being used by Ellen Bulmer of St Mark's Villa in 1878:

Bride Cake

450g/1lb butter	225g/8oz candied lemon peel
450g/1lb sugar	450g/1lb raisins
8 small eggs	700g/1lb 8oz currants
450g/1lb plain flour	100g/4oz chopped blanched almonds
225g/8oz citron, chopped	5ml/1tsp grated nutmeg

Almond Icing

450g/1lb ground almonds	700g/1lb 8oz icing sugar
2 small eggs	100g/4oz apricot jam

Sugar Icing

900g/2lb (approx) icing sugar	5 small egg whites
a few drops of brandy	

1. Prepare a 30cm/12ins, tin as in the previous recipe.
2. Pre-heat the oven to 150°C, 300°F, gas mark 2.
3. Cream the butter with the sugar, beat in the eggs a little at a time, then fold in the flour, the fruit, peel, almonds and nutmeg.
4. Pour the mixture into the tin, and bake for 4 hours 30 mins, to 5 hours.
5. When the cake has been baked, and cooled, make the almond paste by working the almonds and icing sugar with just sufficient beaten egg to form a very firm paste, then heat the apricot jam to boiling, sieve it, and brush it over the cake. Finally roll out the almond paste, apply an even layer all over the cake, and leave it to dry for a few days in a cool, dry place.
6. Beat just sufficient egg white and brandy into the icing sugar to form a Royal icing, and use this to decorate the cake in the usual way.

By this time, however, many people preferred to buy one of the elaborately decorated bride or wedding cakes made by one of the local bakers, who were quite willing and able to offer a complete catering service, thus removing a great burden of trouble, worry (and cash!) from the bride's family. Ladies such as Mrs Thompson of Armley Town Street now took orders for wedding cakes, and all the ices, jellies, creams, etc., required for the wedding breakfast.[5] If it was a society wedding, something

Victorian wedding cakes were extremely ornate, examples like this, made by Higgins and Elliot of Upper Headrow, had each of their three tiers encrusted with moulded sugarwork, modelled foliage, and a range of real, silk, sugar, or embossed gilt foil flowers.

1. *Pre-heat the oven to 170°C, 325°F, gas mark 3.*
2. *Lightly butter either a Swiss Roll tin, or three standard loaf tins, and dust them with a mixture of flour and caster sugar.*
3. *Beat the eggs in a bowl placed over a pan of lukewarm water, then beat in the sugar until the mixture is light in colour, and retains the impression of the whisk after a few seconds, then carefully fold in the sifted flour, and either pour it all into the Swiss Roll tin, or divide one third into each of the bread tins.*
4. *Bake for about 20 minutes, carefully remove on to a cooling rack, and leave it until quite cold.*
5. *Cut the sponges into fingers about an inch wide by about four inches long, and place these on the racks in a cool oven, until they have dried out to perfect crispness.*

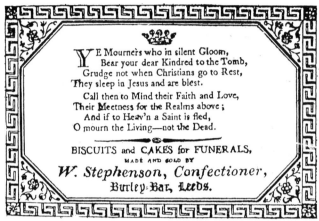

The long sponge finger-biscuits made for funerals were wrapped in paper squares printed with appropriate verses and an advertisement for the confectioner. These are the wrapper designs of W.Stephenson, whose shop was close to the junction of Albion Street and the Headrow around 1816-1825.

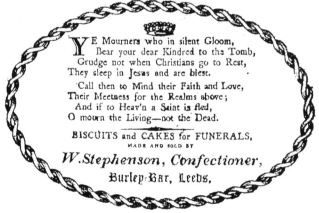

rather more grand would have to be commissioned from the town's leading bride cake manufacturers, Messrs Higgins and Elliot of 2 & 3 Upper Headrow.[6] Founded by Mr Harley in 1858, this company supplied the finest of cakes, all ornately iced in the most ornate High Victorian fashion. Not only that, but they also supplied the turtle, julienne and muligatawny soups, the lemon, orange and maraschino jellies, the trifles, Italian creams, blancmanges, the ice-creams, and every kind of sweet cake and dessert required to make this meal an outstanding and memorable success. The cake itself remained the centrepiece of the whole event, tiny slices, wrapped in a napkin and neatly boxed, being presented to the guests and those who had unfortunately been unable to attend the celebrations.

Distinctive foods also played their part in commemorating the end of life, at the funeral tea. Whenever anyone died, one of the family's first tasks was to order a large supply of funeral biscuits. These were long sponge fingers, made to recipes such as the following example published in Leeds in 1830:[7]

Funeral Biscuits

3 medium free-range eggs	*150g/3oz plain flour*
150g/3oz caster sugar	

These were carefully wrapped in a sheet of printed paper bearing an appropriate verse, perhaps lines from the funeral service, and an advertisement for the confectioner who supplied them.[8] Sealed with a drop of black sealing wax, they were then carried round to the deceased's friends and neighbours by a "bidder", often the undertaker or his assistant in funeral dress, who knocked at the door and announced: "You are expected to attend John Smith's burying tomorrow at three o'clock … We bury at …", then leaving a packet of the biscuits by way of a formal invitation.

At the appointed time, everyone assembled at the deceased's house, or, if there was not sufficient room, in that of a neighbour. In the poorer homes it was expected that each of the mourners would make a small contribution to help cover the costs, a near relative sitting by the open coffin to receive the donations as each visitor came to take a last look at the body before it was committed to the grave. Wine was then handed round, along with more funeral biscuits. Chairs were next carried into the middle of the street, the coffin brought out and sung over before being carried by the bearers, still singing, at a slow march to the top of the street, where the hearse was waiting. Everyone then followed the cortège to the church, only a few "tea-makers" remaining behind to prepare the refreshments ready for their return.[9] These ceremonies had been carried out in a similar way for centuries, Ralph Thoresby, the Leeds historian, recording how on 12 February 1680, he was "All day at Holbeck, assisting to my utmost at dear uncle's funeral: but such a vast multitude, what bidden and unbidden, that abundance of confusion must unavoidably happen (of 130 dozen of cakes [i.e. 1,560!] not one left'. Meanwhile at the funeral of Lord Bathurst's brother on 28 March 1681 "all the company had gloves, with sack and biscuits".[10] These "cakes" were probably identical to the carraway shortcake variety of moulded funeral biscuits which were made in the Dales up to the early 20th century. There were also funeral buns, which, along with ale, formed part of the funeral tea. In 1830 the following recipe for making them was published in Leeds:[11]

H.Spencer's shop was close to the Parish Church, a very convenient place to attract custom for funerals, This funeral biscuit wrapper dates from around 1817.

Funeral Buns

900g/2lb plain flour	*pinch each of ground ginger,*
25g/1oz butter	*cinnamon, & carraway seeds*
25g/1oz sugar	*600ml/1pt milk at blood heat*
75g/3oz currants	*15ml/1tbs rosewater*

25g/1oz fresh yeast (or 15ml/1tbs dried yeast activated according to the manufacturer's instructions)

1. *Rub the butter into the flour, sugar and spices, stir in the currants, and make a well in the centre.*
2. *Stir the yeast and rosewater into the milk until dissolved, then stir it into the flour, etc., adding just sufficient to form a soft dough.*
3. *Turn the dough out on to a floured board and knead for 10 minutes, then place it in a bowl, cover it lightly with a cloth or piece of thin plastic sheet, and leave it in a warm place until doubled in size.*
4. *Turn it out on to a lightly floured board and knead for 2-3 minutes, form it into two large spherical buns, place these on lightly greased baking sheets, cover them lightly once more, and leave them in the warm for about 30 minutes until doubled in size.*
5. *Pre-heat the oven to 200°C, 400°F, gas mark 6, and when the buns are ready, bake them for about 25 minutes.*

The remainder of the tea, which invariably included large quantities of boiled ham, was always of the very best which the family could afford, even if the expense might leave them with considerable debts. This was one of the most important events which they would ever have to arrange, one which involved not only themselves, but all their relations, friends and neighbours who came to pay their respects, to share their memories, and to mourn the dearly departed.

In addition to these special meals which formed an essential element of family life, there were numerous others which marked the progress of the year. The first of these after Christmas and the New Year was:

Slecking-Out Supper

Held by local weavers in late February, this was an ordinary communal supper, followed by the drinking of toasts, which marked the end of the darkest winter months, during which it had been necessary to regularly use artificial light.[12]

Collop Monday

On the Monday before Shrove Tuesday, "collops", slices of bacon, were fried with eggs for the midday meal, the popularity of this custom causing bacon to cost a penny or twopence a pound dearer than normal. This custom, like those of the following days, was originally intended as a way of using up most of the perishable food before the onset of Lent.[13]

Shrove Tuesday

Better known as Pancake Day, the celebrations usually started after the church bells had been rung at 11am, when the school children and the apprentices left their work and every home started to prepare their pancakes. The afternoon was spent in various sports, such as football, shuttlecock and, at Lofthouse, "orange throwing", when three oranges were balanced on sticks and aimed at. Most of these activities had died out by the mid-19th century, only the pancake making continuing through to today.[14]

Pancakes[15]

100g/4oz plain flour	*3ml/½tsp Salt*
3 small eggs	*dripping for frying*
300ml/½pt milk	*lemon juice & sugar*

1. *Mix the flour and salt in a bowl and make a well in the centre.*
2. *Beat the eggs, beat in the milk, and then pour into the flour, beating it with a wooden spoon to produce a smooth batter. Leave this to rest for 30 minutes.*
3. *Melt a little dripping in a frying pan, pour in enough batter just to cover the bottom, and cook on one side, before tossing over and cooking on the other.*
4. *Keep all the pancakes hot. And when all are cooked, serve them sprinkled with sugar and lemon juice.*

Ash Wednesday

Salt fish used to be eaten on this day, but the tradition was already obsolete by the early Victorian period.[16]

Frutters Thursday

The Thursday in Shrove week received this name from the custom of frying "frutterses" or fritters for dinner. Measuring 7-10cm/3-4ins across, they were made to recipes such as the following example published by Ann Peckham in 1773:[17]

To make Drop Fritters

2 eggs	2 medium apples, grated
225g/8oz plain flour	12g/½oz candied peel
25g/1oz fresh yeast	pinch of ground nutmeg
50g/2oz currants	200ml/⅓ pint tepid milk
50g/2oz caster sugar	15ml/1tbs brandy
100g/4oz lard for frying	
For the sauce:	
150ml /¼pt white wine	15ml/1tbs sugar
25g/1oz butter	

1. Dissolve the yeast in the milk and brandy, and pour it into the remainder of the dry ingredients
2. Mix in the eggs before covering, and leaving to rise in a warm place for 2-3 hours.
3. Drop large spoonfuls of the batter into boiling lard in a frying pan, cook light brown on one side and then the other, pile them on a hot plate, and sprinkle them with sugar.
4. Melt the ingredients of the sauce, until very hot, shake them in the pan, and pour into a sauceboat to accompany the fritters.

Palm Sunday

As in other parts of the country, Palm Sunday was celebrated by visits to particular local springs or wells to take their waters, which were supposed to have supernatural powers at this particular time. At St Anne's Well at Howley, for example, it was the custom to throw "palms" (pussy-willow) into the water to attract its miraculous powers of healing. Even in the 1870s thousands of people from all the surrounding villages gathered here every Palm Sunday.[18]

Easter

At Easter-time, in addition to the usual hot-cross bun, every child would look forward to receiving its pace-egg, this being a hen's egg which had been specially hard-boiled and decorated by one of its elder relations or friends. Before dyes were as fast as they are today, a favourite method was to tie a piece of boldly-patterned cloth around the egg and then boil it for an hour or so, thus transferring its colours to the eggshell. Alternatively the eggs could be covered with the brown outer skins of onions firmly bound in place with knitting wool (use a length of old tights today) before being boiled, or else the eggs could be dipped in a dyestuff smuggled from one of the local dyehouses. These customs rapidly fell out of use after the 1940s, since children preferred the gaily wrapped and brightly decorated chocolate Easter eggs which were now available from virtually every corner shop and newsagent throughout the city.

Whitsuntide

This was the great time for Sunday School Whit Walks, as described later on in the chapter on chapel teas.

Bonfire Night, 5 November

For weeks before Bonfire Night, groups of youths called "cadgers" went from house to house begging for coal or "chumps" in the form of stumps, branches, loose railings or fence posts, etc. Old furniture was also disposed of in this way, and even in the 1950s fine long-case clocks, mahogany sofas and half-tester beds, now highly-valued antiques, all came to their untimely end on local bonfires. It was always advisable to give something to the cadgers or chumpers, otherwise lighted squibs or jumping crackers could mysteriously appear in keyholes and under doors late at night.

Having assembled the fire, it was crowned with the traditional Guy, and lit in the early evening, everyone bringing their parkin and bonfire toffee to share with their friends. Then, as John Batty described "the yards were all a-blaze with the towering flames of the monster fires, and the continual noise of firework explosions, and the loud and startling report of cannons and pistols, frightening horses and annoying the sick and nervous".[19]

The parkin, made of oatmeal and treacle, was originally baked as a thick biscuit on the top of a hot bakestone, the following similar version, used by Ellen Bulmer of St Mark's Villa in 1878, being baked on oven sheets:

Parkins

450g/1lb medium oatmeal	2.5ml/½tsp Bicarbonate of soda
50g/2oz dripping or butter	130-175g/5-6oz, black treacle
10ml/2tsp ground ginger	

1. Mix together all the dry ingredients, rub in the fat, then use a knife to work in sufficient treacle to make a stiff paste.
2. Knead the dough until smooth, dusting it with a little more oatmeal, roll out 1cm/half an inch, thick, cut out in rounds, and bake on a lightly-greased oven sheet at 170°C, 320°F, gas mark 3, for 15 minutes, leaving space for them to spread while cooking.

The traditional Yorkshire Parkin was a rich, dark oatmeal slab-cake, often hard when baked, but then mellowing to the most delicious stickiness when stored for a few weeks to "come again":[20]

Yorkshire Parkin

450g/1lb fine oatmeal	5ml/1tsp ground ginger
450g/1lb golden syrup	3ml/½tsp bicarbonate of soda
100g/4oz butter	30ml/2tbs demerara sugar
15ml/1tbs milk	

1. Line a dripping tin with greased greaseproof paper.
2. Pre-heat the oven to 180°C, 350°F, gas mark4.
3. Rub the butter into the oatmeal, and mix in the ginger and sugar.
4. Just melt the treacle in a saucepan, and mix the bicarbonate into the milk, then mix all the ingredients together, pour it into the dripping tin, and bake for about an hour.

Parkin Superbe[21]

150g/6oz medium oatmeal	75g/3oz plain flour
50g/2oz butter	225g/8oz golden syrup
50g/2oz brown sugar	5ml/1tsp ground ginger
3ml/½tsp baking powder	15ml/1tbs rum

1. Rub the butter into the flour and the oatmeal, mix in the sugar, ginger and treacle, then leave to stand overnight.

---

2. Line a dripping tin with greased greaseproof paper.

3. Pre-heat the oven to 180°C, 350°F, gas mark 4.

4. Stir the baking powder and rum into the mixture, pour it into the tin, fork it level, and bake for 50 minutes.

Bonfire night certainly would not have been complete without supplies of hard, dark treacle toffee. This was a "compound of treacle, sugar, vinegar and butter, boiled and spread out in pudding tins till cool, when it is broken up ready for use. On the anniversary of the Gunpowder Plot, the boiling of 'succour' is very general, even amongst the better class of tradespeople."[22]

Treacle Toffee

450g/1lb demerara sugar	15ml/1tbs vinegar
100g/4oz butter	15ml/1tbs water
100g/4oz golden syrup or black treacle	15ml/1tbs milk

1. Grease a shallow baking tray or dripping tin.

2. Gently boil together all the ingredients except the vinegar, for 15-20 minutes, stirring continuously until it becomes brittle when dropped into cold water.

3. Stir in the vinegar, pour into the prepared tin, and allow to cool until it has set solid.

St Thomas' Day, 21 December

As the shortest day of the year, this was the traditional time for giving charitable donations just before Christmas. Up to around 1830 poor families would go to local farmers, who would give them a peck (16 pints) of corn which, at Rothwell, Jenny Dawson the miller would grind free of charge.[23] Some wheat would also be kept whole ready for making frumenty for Christmas Eve.

From St Thomas' Day, preparations for Christmas went on apace. Butchers' shops had their windows and frontages festooned with all the beef, ham, poultry, pies, etc., which would be needed over the coming holiday, while grocers displayed all their wares both in their shops, and along the pavement before their doors. This was certainly a great way of advertising, but was hardly hygienic. My great-grandmother did not buy her Christmas cheese from one local shop in the 1890s, having seen a neighbour's dog cock its leg against a large show of cheeses displayed in this way! It was also customary for the grocers and general provision dealers to give Christmas boxes of cake, cheese and a glass of gin or rum to their regular customers, along with a large blue mould-candle for use on Christmas Eve. Meanwhile in the inns and taverns, where business was particularly brisk at this time, the publicans bought in a stock of game and other festive food as a raffle prize for their customers. Usually between 100 and 150 one shilling (5p) tickets were sold, the prize, known as "Christmas Cheer" being drawn on the Saturday preceding the great day.[24]

This was also the time for Christmas parties, held in the evenings in many homes. Richard Spencer has left an excellent description of one of these events in a skilled working-class house most probably around Holbeck. By the time the guests were expected, a white cloth had been laid on a long table in the front room, and the urn, teapots, cups and saucers, and

In Edwardian Leeds Richard Boston & Sons' Christmas display was one of the great sights of Boar Lane. Their shop stocked everything for good living, including fish, game, venison, poultry, choice early fruit and vegetables, Royal Whitstable oysters, Italian warehouse goods, and even blocks of pure natural ice specially imported from America by the Wenham Lake Ice Company. *(Leeds Library)*.

decanters full of temperance wines set in place, while in the middle of the table:

> There was plumcake, and seedcake, on gilt china plates,
> Nice teacakes, and hot buttered muffins,
> There were spongebuns, and rice-loaf, and fine pickled shrimps,
> Of ham sandwiches, too, a prime lot:
> Tea-biscuits, with rich orange marmalade on,
> And a great many things I can't dwell upon,
> And plenty I've really forgot'

As they arrived, gentlemen handed chairs for the ladies, until all were seated in couples around the table, and the meal began. Afterwards the ladies cleared the china, and the men removed the table and urn, and set the chairs around the perimeter of the room, ready for playing games of Postman's Knock, spinning the trencher, peepshow games, kissing through chairs, and love ribbons, all great party games, some of them centuries old, and which only petered out in the 1950s. Finally the party broke up around 11.30pm, when the guests left, having passed a memorable evening in great comfort and fun, and with anticipation of similar evenings to come.

Now it was time to take a quantity of whole wheat, place it in a clean bag, and beat it with a wooden rolling pin at the top of the cellar steps to remove the husks. For home use, it was then placed in a large pan of water and simmered very slowly to "cree" the wheat over the next 24 hours, until it had swollen into a thick, soft, glutinous mass. This was the "ancient and honest method, creed wheat, an' nut flour porridge, an' gooas a good deal farther", for the creed wheat sold in the shops was bulked out with flour, with a saving of threequarters of the grain. The mixture was then poured into basins, allowed to cool until set, turned out, and piled up in jelly-like cakes in the shop windows ready for sale.

Christmas Eve

A major task, along with completing the shopping and cleaning the house, was to use the creed wheat to make a dish called frumenty, this word coming from the Latin *frumentum* meaning corn. It probably originated in prehistoric times, as the basic way of making the gathered wild seeds more palatable and nutritive. It was popular throughout the medieval period too, and is still made by some Yorkshire families even today. To convert the creed wheat into frumenty, it was boiled with milk, sugar and spices, as in this version:[25]

Frumenty

600ml/1pt pearled wheat	sugar to taste
600ml/1pt milk	grated cinnamon, nutmeg
900ml/1½pt water	or allspice to taste
100g/4oz currants	

1. Place the grain and water in a large lidded ovenproof casserole, and place either in a moderate oven or in a pan of simmering water on the hob, for about 24 hours, or, alternatively, bring it to the boil in a lidded saucepan, and wrap it in blankets for 8-12 hours before re-heating and wrapping it once more, thus causing the grain to "cree" into a thick jelly-like mass.
2. Add the milk and currants, boil for 10-15 minutes, sweeten and add spices to taste, stirring in a little flour and water at this stage if it is rather too thin.
3. Serve very hot, accompanied by small jugs of cream or cold milk.

A rather richer version made from pearl barley instead of wheat was also being made here in the 1740s.[26]

To Make Plumb Gruel

100g/4oz pearl barley	100g/4oz currants
2.5l/3pts water	100g/4oz raisins
2 blades of mace	60ml/4tbs white wine
finely peeled zest of a ½ lemon	3ml/½tsp ground nutmeg
juice of a ½ lemon	45ml/3tbs sugar

1. Slowly simmer the barley, mace and lemon peel in the water for about 1-1½ hours until thick and tender, stirring from time to time to prevent it from burning.
2. Add the currants and raisins, continue cooking for about 30 minutes until they have plumped up, then add the remaining ingredients, and serve hot.

In the evening, all the family would gather at their home, now decorated with fir, rosemary, holly, laurel and box. The blue Yule candle, also decorated with evergreens, was then lit using a long paper taper, and allowed to burn without snuffing, for it was most important that the charred wick should always remain intact. For this reason it was never blown out, but the flame extinguished by being nipped between the jaws of a pair of tongs. The Yule clog, or log, was then placed on the fire, and lit with a strip of the previous clog, carefully preserved from the last Christmas Eve. The family then sat down to their supper, which included the frumenty, with spice cake and cheese, etc.[27]

Christmas Day, 25 December

In some households the Yule clog ceremony actually took place on Christmas Day, as described in J. N. Dickinson's memories of Christmas in Leeds around 1830: "On Christmas Day a few of my late father's workmen would give the master a call in the forenoon, when spice-cake, cheese and ale were partaken of, the foreman, in return, wishing him and his family the compliments of the season. Houses were then as now decorated with holly, mistletoe, etc., principally in the windows …At dinner-time, roast beef (turkeys belonged to the "upper ten"), plum pudding (I am afraid with brandy sauce), mince tarts, and custards were served. During the evening the "yule log" was placed on the fire instead of coal: and where there was a large family, games of various kinds were introduced and occasionally, very occasionally, dancing allowed. At supper-time toasted cheese and "swig" was served. The latter consisted of toasted bread well sprinkled with various spices and placed in a bowl of hot ale. As a rule all festivities were over by ten o'clock and the household were soon after in bed.[28]

In other households slightly different customs were observed, one writer remembering how on Christmas morning children went to the houses of those their mother knew, and called through the keyhole:

> Ah wish yuh a merry Kersamas, a happy New Year,
> A pocket full o'money, an' a barril full o'beer.
> Please will yuh gie muh mah Kersamas b-o-x!'

If no one else had let in Christmas (provided that they were not girls, and, if possible, were not red-headed either) they were let in and given bread, cheese, and always money, in return for which they left a sprig or two of evergreens. It was customary to keep open house on Christmas Day, all visitors having bread and cheese set before them, from which they could help themselves.[29]

Now was the time to prepare the Christmas dinner, for which the main course was traditionally a large joint of roast beef, many people going to Leeds market late on the evening of Christmas Eve, as butchers then had to drop their prices in order to sell all their meat before the onset of the holiday. By the 1860s, it was reported that the joints of beef "were a shadow of what they were. The flocks of geese which were walked into the town on the preceding day are an indication of the revolution in taste", [30] and since then most families tried to provide poultry for their Christmas dinner. For the second course, there was the inevitable Christmas pudding, made perhaps weeks before, and which had been put on to boil early on Christmas morning. Up to the mid-19th century the puddings were of a relatively plain, lightly-fruited variety, but as the expanding overseas trade brought in cheaper supplies of dried fruits they became much richer, sweeter and darker, as may be seen in this example. [31]

A Rich Plum Pudding, 1883

700g/1lb 8oz raisins	*225g/8oz plain flour*
450g/1lb currants	*450g/1lb suet*
225/8oz candied orange peel	*15ml/1tbs ground nutmeg*
225/8oz candied citron peel	*9 medium eggs*
350g/12oz fresh breadcrumbs	*large pinch ground cinnamon*

1. Mix the dry ingredients, make a well in the centre, beat the eggs with the milk, work this mixture into the dry ingredients, mixing in just sufficient water to form a soft dough.

2. Scald a piece of muslin, sprinkle it with flour, shake off the surplus, lay it over a basin, put in the pudding, tie the muslin tightly over it, lift the pudding from the bowl plunge it into a pan of boiling water and boil for three hours.

A traditional Christmas pudding, boiled for hours in a saucepan or in the set pot, and served with a sweet brandy sauce, and a sprig of holly.

The apparently simple act of boiling a pudding could lead to complete disaster in the hands of an inexperienced cook, as the Holbeck poet Richard Spencer described in this poem: [32]

The Christmas Pudding

Thear raisins, curns, an lemon peel
Quite fill'd an ample traay,
Fer t'Chistmas puddin' they'd ta boil
That neet fer Christmas daay:
An varry sooin 'twer nicely shaped
Then inta t'pot it went:
Wal t'bubblin', steamin' watter show'd
'Twer bizness 'at it meant.

Nah, genuine Christmas Puddins need
Sum haars, they saay, ta boil
Soa Sam fetch'd up, wah, nearly hauf

A hundredweight o'coil,
Fer he'd agreed ta mind this thing
Wal t'wife retired ta rest:
Hiz job were simple, an he thowt
He'd manage it wi' t'best.

Well, t'puddin heaved an, roll'd i' t'pot:
He'd sich a roarin fire,
Fer feedin it wi" extra coils
He nivver seem'd ta tire …
Bud midneet fun him varry tired:
Poor Sam, he fell asleep,
Then fun all t'watter'd boil'd awaay,
An t'thing begun ta baak.

Fer wen he mustered courage up
To lewk inta t'set pot,
He hardly cud believe his ees,
He fun the thing red-hot
They might as weel at t'first i" t'oven
Av baaked that dainty doaf,
They ne'er dreamt Christmas puddin, ud
Turn aght a Christmas loaf!

After the pudding had been served, flaming with brandy and accompanied by sweet white sauce flavoured with rum or brandy, there might be a few hours of relaxation, conversation, reading and play, before high tea, with its cold meats, pork pie, spice or Christmas cakes and minced pies. The spice cake was originally a fairly light yeast-raised fruit loaf, and women used to make a point of obtaining a piece of spice-cake from each of their friends, for each piece was believed to give them a "happy-month" in the coming year. [33] During the later Victorian period, however, it developed into the richly fruited and highly ornamented iced Christmas cake we still enjoy today, always eaten with Wensleydale or similar white cheese in the true Yorkshire manner. The following recipe was published by Amy Atkinson and Grace Holroyd in Leeds in 1909:

A Rich Christmas Cake

325g/11oz butter	*100g/4oz blanched, flaked almonds*
325g/11oz plain flour	*225g/8oz candied peel*
275g/10oz caster sugar	*30ml/2tbs brandy*
450g/1lb raisins	*6 eggs, beaten*
450g/1lb currants	*15ml/1tbs mixed spice*

1. Line a 25cm/9ins round tin with greased greaseproof paper, and tie three layers of brown paper or newspaper around the outside as extra insulation.

2. Beat the butter, cream in the sugar, then beat in the eggs, little by little, alternately with the flour, then mix in the remaining ingredients in small quantities.

3. Pre-heat the oven to 170°C, 325°F, gas mark 3, pour the mixture into the tin, and bake for 3 hours 30 min – 4 hours.

As their name suggests, the mince pies were originally made of minced beef or mutton flavoured with a few currants, sugar and spices, but by the mid 18th century they had already begun to resemble their modern sweet, meatless successors. In 1773 Ann Peckham still included a complete set of calves feet in her recipes, and J. E. Thomas' 1830 version used shredded par-boiled tongue. [34] However, in all the following versions the meat has disappeared, except for the suet, so that they may still be made today, using vegetarian suet if this is preferred.[35]

Minced Pies, 1741

100g/4oz ground almonds	*100g/4oz candied peel*
10ml/2tsp rosewater	*100g/4oz sugar*
225g/8oz suet	*15ml/2oz brandy*
100g/4oz minced apples	*pinch of ground mace*
225g/8oz currants	*pinch of salt*

Minced Pies, 1840s

450g/1lb suet	*5ml/1tsp ground nutmeg*
225g/8oz chopped apples	*5ml/1tsp ground mace*
225g/8oz currants	*5ml/1tsp ground cinnamon*
225g/8oz raisins	*5ml/1tsp salt*
75g/3oz chopped blanched almonds	*45ml/3tbs brandy*
50g/2oz candied peel	*60ml/4tbs white wine*
45ml/3tbs sugar	

1. Mix the ingredients of either version together, and use to fill covered mince pies made with either puff or shortcrust pastry, brushing their tops with milk and sprinkling them with sugar.

2. Bake at 220°C, 425°F, gas mark 7 for 15-20 minutes, until golden brown.

In the wealthier households, those of the aristocracy, the merchants and bankers, pies of a much more substantial nature were made. These were the famous Yorkshire Christmas Pies, made with geese, turkeys and other birds, boned, seasoned, wrapped one within another, and baked in an enormous piecrust. Elizabeth Moxon's 1740s version was fairly simple, with a turkey stuffed with a chicken and forcemeat, surrounded by forcemeat balls, baked in a pastry-covered pie dish and then, with the lid removed, garnished with stewed oysters and fried artichoke bottoms. Ann Peckham's 1767 version is much more typical:[36]

To make a Yorkshire Christmas Pie

Raise a pretty strong crust, bone a goose, a turkey, a fowl, a partridge, a pigeon, season them with half an ounce of mace, half an ounce of nutmeg, an equal quantity of salt, half an ounce of white pepper, all beat fine together, wrap them one within another, and the goose on the outside, lay them in the crust, so as it will look like one goose: take a hare wiped clean with a cloth, cut in pieces, and lay it as close as you can on one side, and on the other woodcock, moorgame [grouse], or what sort of wild fowl you can get, season them well and put butter over them: then lay on a thick lid, and let it be well baked: when it is taken out of the oven, fill it with clarified butter: before you put it in the oven take some strong paper doubled and buttered and bind about the sides, which is a great support to a raised crust, and keeps the ornament from burning.

Even in the 1890s, these pies were still being baked for Christmas at Harewood House, probably using the great embossed copper raised-pie mould which still remains in the kitchens there today. This recipe was almost certainly written by the Earl of Harewood's chef de cuisine, M. Louis Lecompte, one of the greatest chefs of his day.[37]

In most parts of Yorkshire "goose-pie" is a favourite food of the season, and it is very good eating too, as may be proved by manufacturing a sample from one of the recipes ...for the genuine article, which forms an important feature of the Yorkshire Christmas festivities. It is made as follows:

A Yorkshire Christmas Pie, made to the Harewood recipe, in the Harewood mould, contained a chicken wrapped inside a goose, and a variety of game, all packed in a rich forcemeat within an elaborately moulded piecrust.

Yorkshire Pie

Bone a large fowl and fill the body with a stuffing made of 1 teacupful of minced lamb or tongue, 1 breakfastcup full of minced veal, 1 teacupful of finely chopped suet, 2 tablespoonfuls of chopped parsley, pepper and salt freely to taste, massed together with 2 beaten eggs: or the following stuffing may be used: The same quantities of minced ham or tongue, veal and suet, 1 table-spoonful of powdered sweet herbs, a finely-chopped partly-boiled onion, 1 teaspoonful of grated lemon peel, half a teaspoonful of mixed ground spices, 2 teaspoonfuls of salt, and half a saltspoonful of cayenne pepper, worked into a paste with two large beaten eggs.

Sew up the fowl, truss it to a good shape, and then stew it with the goose in a close stewpan, moistening with some good stock. After stewing for half-an-hour, take the fowl and goose out of the stewpan, fold the fowl up in the goose, and lay the two in a pie-mould which has been lined with a good pie-paste, having previously put a layer of the same stuffing as used for the fowl at the bottom of the pie. Pack round the goose slices of partly-boiled tongue and pieces of pigeon, partridge, hare, or any other game to hand. Fill up the gaps with more stuffing, and pour in as much as possible of the stock in which the goose or fowl were stewed. Spread a quarter-inch layer of butter over the contents, cover it with paste, ornament as desired, brush over the top of the pie with white of egg, and bake in a slow oven for three hours.

When this pie was recently made in the original mould at Harewood House, it was the epitome of succulent texture and fine flavour, confirming its reputation as the finest of all the great English raised pies.

Rich and expensive food of this quality was clearly beyond the means of most families, but even in the new 1858-61 Workhouse on Beckett Street, now the Thackray Medical Museum at Jimmy's, the Leeds Board of Guardians tried to give a good time to its inmates. On Christmas Day in the Leeds Workhouse "both the establishment and its character were changed. Where stern order usually ruled, supervised by naked gauntness, the emblems of mirth were evident. To the inmates of the Workhouse proper dinner was served in the large dining hall, looking bright and cheerful with mottoes, texts, designs and festoons. Close upon 470 men and women had a dinner of roast beef and plumb pudding with coffee at the close. By the hearty appetites of the diners there were disposed of 46 stones of beef, 6 of suet, 37 of potatoes, and the pudding contained 100lb of plums, 50lb of currants and 40lb of sultanas. Sweets and tobacco came afterwards, and an entertainment of a 'free and easy' character appropriately ended an enjoyable day."[38]

Twelfth Night Eve, 5 January

"In that part of Yorkshire, near Leeds, where I was born and spent my youth," wrote Josiah Beckwith, "I remember when I was a boy [about 1700] that it was customary for many families on the eve of the twelfth day of Christmas to invite their relations, friends and neighbours to their houses to play at cards and to partake of a supper, of which minced pies were an indispensable ingredient: and after supper was brought in the Wassail Cup or Wassail Bowl, being a large bowl. A plate of spiced cake was first handed round to the company, and then the Wassail Bowl, of which everyone partook by taking with a spoon out of the ale a roasted apple, and eating it, and then drinking the health of the company out of the Bowl, wishing them a merry Christmas and a happy New Year. The ingredients of the bowl was usually called Lambswool."[39]

The same wassail bowl, decorated with sprays of evergreen, was probably carried around the streets by groups of young girls who sang their wassail carol and offered a drink to those who rewarded them with a small gift of money. By the mid-19th century the bowl and its contents had disappeared completely, Only the bough of greenery, the wassail bob, decorated with oranges, ornaments, and a wax representation of the infant Jesus, remained. This was carried round the streets hidden beneath a cloak, the girls attracting their gifts by singing the traditional Leeds song:

'Here we come a-wassailing,
Among the leaves so green, [i.e.,the decorations of the wassail bowl]
Here we come a-wandering,

So fair to be seen.
Chorus: Love and joy come to you
    And to you your wassail too,
    And God bless you and send you a happy New Year
    And God send you a happy New Year.
Our wassail cup is made
Of the rosemary tree,
And so is your beer
Of the best barley …'

By the early 20th century all memories of the original wassailing had disappeared from general memory, and so it was imagined that this word, being associated with Christmas, must have a religious meaning, and so the decorations of the wassail bob became nonconformatised as Wesley Bobs, the local name for the decorations used to adorn the Christmas trees. However, to celebrate both the end of the 12 days of Christmas, and the end of the annual cycle of customs and celebrations, the following recipe for lambswool may be tried, using a traditional Otley version of mulled ale as a base.[40]

Lambswool

100g/4oz sugar (approx)	*100g/4oz brown sugar*
6 eating apples	*20ml/4tsp ground ginger*
1½pt strong brown ale	*120ml/8tbs rum or brandy*

pinch each of ground cinnamon and cloves

1. *Core the apples, fill them with sugar, place them in a baking dish with a little water, and cook for 45-60 minutes at 190°C, 375°F, gas mark 5, until tender.*
2. *Just before serving put all the remaining ingredients, except the rum or brandy, into a saucepan, bring it to the boil, pour it into a bowl, stir in the rum or brandy, put in the apples, and serve immediately.*

Thus fortified, everyone really was ready to start the coming year.

Notes:

1. H. A. Cadman, *Gomersal Past & Present,* Armley (1930) 113
2. J. Lawson, *Progress in Pudsey,* Stanningley (1887) 8
3. A. Peckham, *The Complete English Cook,* Leeds (1773) 105
4. J. E. Thomas, *New Whole Art of Confectionery,* Leeds (1830) 19
5. T. Kirkby, *Armley Through the Camera,* Armley (1901) 55
6. Anon., *Industries of Yorkshire,* (1888) 78
7. Thomas, *op.cit.,* 13
8. P. Brears, *Traditional Food in Yorkshire,* Edinburgh (1987) 192-6
9. Anon., *Dialect of Leeds,* (1862) 260
10. J. Hunter (ed.), *The Diary of Ralph Thoresby,* (1830)
11. Thomas, *op.cit.,* 10
12. Anon., *Dialect of Leeds,* (1862) 41
13. *ibid.,* 272
14. W. Smith, *The History of Morley,* (1876) 91 & J. Batty, *The History of Rothwell,* Rothwell (1877) 216
15. A. Atkinson & G.Holroyd, *Practical Cookery,* Leeds (6th ed.1909) 170
16. W. Smith, *op.cit.,* 91
17. Anon., *Dialect of Leeds,* (1862)307 & A. Peckham, *op.cit.,* 130
18. W. Smith, *op.cit.,* 92
19. J. Batty, *op.cit.,* 27
20. Atkinson & Holroyd, *op.cit.,* 148 & 151
21. *ibid.,* 151
22. Anon., *Dialect of Leeds:* & P. Brears, *op.cit.,* 161
23. J. Batty, *op.cit.,* 217
24. Anon., *Dialect of Leeds,* (1862) 263-4
25. *ibid.,* 306
26. E. Moxon, *English Housewifery Exemplified,* Leeds (c.1749) 143
27. Anon., *Dialect of Leeds,* (1862) 264
28. *Local Notes & Queries,* no.520 (1888)
29. Anon., *Dialect of Leeds,* (1862) & J. Batty, *op.cit.,* 215
30. Anon., *Dialect of Leeds,* (1862)
31. J. E. Thomas, *op.cit.,* 36, & *Leeds Mercury Supplement,* 20/12/1883
32. R. Spencer, *Field Flowers,* Batley (1890)
33. Anon., *Dialect of Leeds,* (1862) 264
34. A. Peckham, *op.cit.,* 107 & J. E. Thomas, *op.cit.,* 30
35. E. Moxon, *op.cit., 207* & MS cookery book of Susannah Walker, 1833, Leeds Reference Library SR/641.5/W15W
36. E. Moxon, *op.cit.,* 65 & A. Peckham, *op.cit.,* 104
37. T. Garret, *Encyclopaedia of Practical Cookery,* (1890) I 384 & II 803
38. P. Brears, *The Leeds Christmas Book,* Leeds (c.1980) 5
39. *Gentleman's Magazine,* (1784) pt1, 98-9
40. W. C. Platts, *Between Ling and Lowland,* (1901)

GEORGIAN MERCHANTS' GOOD LIVING

WHEN the weavers had heard the market bell sound in Briggate, they had each stepped out of the inns and placed their pieces of cloth on one of the long trestle benches which ran down both sides of the street. Then the merchants arrived, carrying their order books, samples, and small wooden whisks with which to examine each piece, then whispering a price to the weaver, and if it was accepted, noting it down carefully. In this way some £10-12,000-worth of cloth was sold in little more than an hour, the weavers then carrying the cloth on their shoulders to the warehouses and workshops located behind the merchants' grand town houses, such as those which can be seen in Blayds Yard and Queen's Court off Lower Briggate. The merchants then undertook the final finishing processes, which added the real value to the cloth, and arranged its sale and delivery to every fair and market town in the country, and to the London factors for both the metropolitan trade, and for export to America, Russia and Scandinavia. Alternatively, many of the Leeds merchants exported their cloth directly to Holland, Germany, Austria, Spain, and the Baltic ports. In the 1770s up to £1,500,000 of cloth was being exported in just a single year, this trade bringing in great profits, the Leeds merchants now being amongst the wealthiest in the land.

Their town houses and their villas in the suburbs were of the highest standards, designed by architects such as William Etty or John Carr of York, their interiors being beautifully panelled, wallpapered or painted with scenes from classical mythology, and furnished in the most tasteful manner. Guests visiting Croft Preston's house at Town End, the upper end of North Street, would pass through the hall, with its spinnet, into the dining room, hung with paintings and furnished with ten caned dining chairs, its table spread with damask linen, silver and pewter tableware, and steel knives and forks.[1] After dinner, they could then retire to the drawing room, with its needlework chairs, stools, screens and card table, its china and delftware, its tea tables and the tea kettle, lamp and stand used to supply hot water to the two teapots, coffee pots, sugar dish, milk pan and tea spoons, all this equippage being made of solid silver.

As for food preparation, there were beer and wine vessels, meat salting tubs, and a flour boulter or "meal ringing box" in the cellar, and a full set of brewing, baking and washing utensils in the back kitchen. The main kitchen, meanwhile, contained absolutely everything which the cook would need to make the finest meals. There was a cleaver, a chopping knife, a grater and a brass mortar and pestle to prepare the food, a fireplace equipped with fenders, pokers, fire shovels, and tongs, as well as briggs and a pot hook to support pots over the fire, and a chafing dish, a toasting jack, a grid iron and a frying pan for cooking meats etc. Both poultry and joints could be roasted on the spits turning on a pair of racks, their juices being caught in an iron dripping pan, and poured back over the meat with a basting ladle. There was also a plate warmer, to ensure that all the meals were eaten piping hot.

This quality of resources was by no means unique, being found in dozens of merchants' houses throughout the town. On 24 June 1777, for example, the *Leeds Mercury* advertised a house newly-built in Park Row which enjoyed "all convenient Offices. The Kitchen, Laundry, Pantries, Cellars and Servants Hall are fitted up with Strong Ranges, Copper and Set-Pots, [charcoal-heated cooking] Stoves, Smoak-Jack, Shelves, Stone Tables, Sinks, Stone Gantles [beer barrel stands], Binns for Wine, etc. The Butler and Housekeeper's Rooms with Tables and Cases for China and Glasses, a large Dresser with Drawers and a convenient small-Oven, The Dining and Drawing Rooms elegantly fitted up with Marble Chimney-Pieces, beautifully carved …and very fashionable Paper."[2]

In the larger mansions and villas, there were two kitchens, a back kitchen or scullery for the dirtier, wetter processes, and the main kitchen for most of the cooking and also perhaps to serve as a minor servants hall, all these being at ground level. The main kitchens were large rooms, the kitchen at Springfield House measuring 24 by 18ft, with a 12ft 6ins high ceiling, and a suite of back kitchen, pantry, and a large store room, etc.[3] In the smaller houses and terraces the kitchens were increasingly placed in the basements. Here the servants usually entered by flights of stone steps which descended from the street into a paved sunken yard or area, which gave access to the kitchen door, as may be seen in the houses lining the south side of York Place. In John Bilbrough's 1892 sketch of the basement of his home at 2, Preston Place, we can see just how one of these rooms was furnished.[4] The kitchen table beneath the large shuttered window, the long-case clock, the three-legged table

This sketch by John Bilbrough shows the cellar-kitchen at his home at 2, Preston Place, now part of Leeds University. Compared to most ground-floor kitchens, they were rather low-ceilinged. a mid 19th century Leeds opinion being that "them that invented tall hats and cellar-kitchens ought to be smothered"!

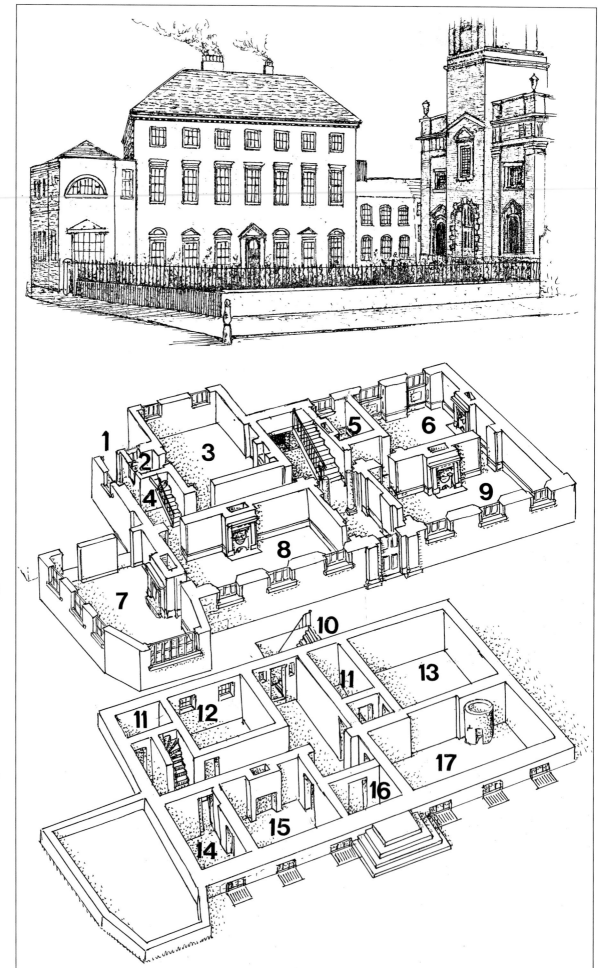

John Dixon's house on Boar Lane was built at a cost of £4,500 in 1750. It incorporated all the service rooms required for maintaining an elegant lifestyle, including:

Ground Floor
1. Back Door
2. Scullery
3. Kitchen
4. Back stairs
5. Butler's Pantry
6. Breakfast Room
7. Banking Hall
8. Dining Room
9. Drawing Room

Cellar
10. Cellar steps from back yard
11. Wine cellar
12. Larder
13. Coal place
14. Mangle room
15. Laundry
16. Ale cellar
17. Brewhouse

and the dresser bearing the standing toaster, copper tea urn and selection of cooking pots, all appear to date from the early 1820s, when the house was built by Captain & Mrs William Lyddon. Later improvements included a mid-19th century range with an oven to one side and a boiler to the other, a pendant gas light, and a bell-system operated by cranks and wires.

To carry out the actual cooking in these households an experienced cook/housekeeper was usually employed, one who had been trained either by working with her predecessors, or who had perhaps received further instruction from a local cookery school, such as the one advertised in the *Leeds Mercury* on 18 March 1777:

"James Mackay, Pastry-Cook, Cook and Confectioner from Bath and London, late Foreman to Mr John Tinsdale, Confectioner, Briggate, Leeds, Begs leave to acquaint the Ladies and Gentlemen of Leeds That he has opened a School for the Instruction of Young Ladies at Mrs Smith's, Confectioner, the Sign of the Golden Sugar Loaf, Upper-Head-Row."

For the best recipes and advice on planning menus, aspiring cooks and the ladies who employed them could purchase one of the fine recipe books specially published in Leeds for their benefit. The first of these, *English Housewifery Exemplified*, written by Mrs Elizabeth Moxon of Pontefract, was published on a subscription basis in 1741, being printed by James Lister and sold by J.Swale in Leeds, with other outlets in Wakefield and Pontefract. It commenced with a series of 458 detailed recipes arranged in the order in which they would be served, with soups, meat, poultry and game, fish, puddings, etc., then becoming more disorganised as it proceeded through pastries, cakes, creams, custards, flummeries and syllabubs, vegetables, preserves and wines, etc. A complete index ensured that each recipe could quickly be found, however. She also provided a menu or bill of fare for dinners and suppers for every month of the year using only those ingredients which would be available at the appropriate season. By any standards, the range of her dishes represents extremely good living, and it is not surprising that Mrs Moxon's volume became one of the most popular cookery books of the 18th century, going into 13 editions in Leeds, with two further editions in London, and another in Hull, the last appearing in 1800.[5]

The second cookery book to be published in Leeds was Ann Peckham's *The Complete English Cook* of 1767. Mrs Peckham lived with her husband in Lydgate, near the Woodhouse Bar, on the site of the present St John's Centre. She apparently attended St John's church, the baptisms and burials of their children appearing in the registers there from the 1730s. Her four sons, Samuel, Thomas, Joseph and Benjamin, along with their daughter Ann, all died in early infancy, only their daughter Elizabeth reaching adulthood, dying unmarried of "a decline" in February 1799. As for Ann herself, she must have published her book towards the end of her life, setting down recipes gathered and tried over many years. On 6 October 1770, the St John's registers simply record the burial of "Wife of Thomas Peckham, Lydgate", the *Leeds Mercury* reporting three days later, "On Thursday last died at her house in Leeds Mrs Peckham, one of the most experienced cooks in this neighbourhood." Her husband died two years later, but apparently their grave remained unmarked, for no Peckham memorial stone was to be found there in 1900.[6]

Mrs Peckham stated that she had gained her experience as

English Housewifry.

EXEMPLIFIED

In above four Hundred and Fifty

RECEIPTS,

Giving DIRECTIONS in most Parts of COOKERY; and how to prepare various Sorts of

SOOPS,	CAKES,
MADE-DISHES,	CREAMS,
PASTS,	JELLIES,
PICKLES,	MADE-WINES,&c.

With CUTS for the orderly placing the DISHES and COURSES; also Bills of Fare for every Month in the Year; and an Alphabetical INDEX of the Whole.

A Book necessary for Mistresses of Families, higher and lower Women Servants, and confined to Things USEFUL, SUBSTANTIAL and SPLENDID, and calculated for the Preservation of HEALTH, and upon the Measures of FRUGALITY, being the Result of thirty Years *Practice* and *Experience.*

By ELIZABETH MOXON.

The FOURTH EDITION.

LEEDES:

Printed by *James Lister*; and sold by the AUTHOR at *Pontefract*, and J. SWALE, Bookseller in *Leeds.*

Elizabeth Moxon's *English Housewifery Exemplified* was first published in 1741, and went on to become one of the most popular cookery books of the 18th century.

"the result of above 40 years' practice in the best families in and about LEEDS", so that her book was "not stuff'd with a nauseous hodge-podge of French kicksaws: and yet the real delicacies of the most sumptuous entertainments are by no means neglected". Her purpose was to advise all ranks of society how to prepare and serve their food in the most elegant, economical, nourishing and wholesome manner, but she especially recommended her book to "such mistresses as think it a burden to be continuously dangling after their maids in the kitchen [so that they] may be exempted in great a measure from that trouble, by putting these rules into the hands of their servants: for special care is taken to make every thing easy and intelligible to the meanest understudy." Her 585 recipes were arranged in a far more orderly manner than Mrs Moxon's, and she took advantage both of some of Mrs Moxon's recipes, along with others taken from cookery books published in the intervening years by Mrs Raffald of Manchester, for example, to satisfy the most fashionable tastes. Her dinner and supper menus are more elaborate too, with nine to 11 dishes to most of her courses, but with 23 dishes for her July meals, and a spectacular 35 for those in December. These really do reflect the growing prosperity and sophistication of the Leeds cloth merchants, for which five editions of her book were published between 1767 and 1790.

THE
Complete Englifh COOK;
OR,
PRUDENT HOUSEWIFE.

BEING,

An entire New Collection of the moft general, yet leaft expenfive RECEIPTS in every Branch of

COOKERY and GOOD HOUSEWIFERY,

With DIRECTIONS for

Roafting,	Fricafeys,	Potting,
Boiling,	Pies, Tarts,	Candying,
Stewing,	Puddings,	Collaring,
Ragoos,	Cheefe-Cakes,	Pickling,
Soups,	Cuftards,	Preferving,
Sauces,	Jellies,	Made-Wines, &c.

Together with Directions for placing Difhes on Tables of Entertainment: And many other Things equally neceffary. The whole made eafy to the meaneft Capacity, and far more ufeful to young Beginners than any Book of the Kind extant.

By ANN PECKHAM, of LEEDS,

Who is well known to have been for Forty Years paft on of the moft noted Cooks in the County of YORK.

The SECOND EDITION.

LEEDS:

Printed (by Affignment from the Author) for GRIFFITH WRIGHT and JOHN BINNS: And fold by S. CROWDER and G. ROBINSON, in Pater-nofter-Row, London, and all other Bookfellers in Town and Country

[Price Two SHILLINGS Bound]

Ann Peckham had the reputation of being one of the region's most experienced cooks. In 1767 she wrote this book at her home in Lydgate, where the St John's Centre now stands, towards the end of forty years cooking for the town's major families.

Evidence that meals of this kind were actually eaten is provided by the following menu prepared for a dinner served to celebrate the Christening of George Skirrow Beecroft of Kirkstall Forge in 1809:[7]

1st Course

Top dish:	Salmon, 8 or 9lbs
Bottom dish:	3 or 4 soles
Other dishes:	Calf's Head, with the leather on to come on Wednesday to be hashed in the French Style
	A Saddle of Mutton
	3 fine fowls
	A Ham
	A couple of fat Ducks
	A Roast Pig
At one corner:	Veal Patties
At the opposite corner:	A breast of Lamb

2nd Course

Leveret and plumb Pudding, Four Fresh Calf's feet to be boiled on Wednesday, to be made strong for Jelly. Half a dozen oranges for a new dish. Also to be ordered a pint of cream and two

quarts of milk for other sweets, etc., etc., Stilton cheese and celery to be handed round.
These were followed by bumpers of good wine, home brewed ale, etc.

As the above menu shows, the main meals were carefully planned, the place of each dish on the table being decided beforehand. This is because they were to be served in the traditional manner, known as à la Française, with only two courses, each one including a large number of varied dishes, from which the diners could help themselves, or each other.

A Dinner in Winter.   Second Courfe.   A Supper in Winter.

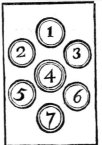

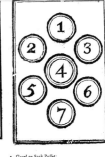

1. A Soop.	1. A Turkey.	1. Gruel or Sack Poffet.
2. Scotch Collops.	2. Almond Cheefe-Cakes.	2. Tarts.
3. Boil'd Chickens.	3. Sturgeon.	3. Lobfter.
4. Stew'd Oyfters or roafted Lobfter.	4. Partridges.	4. Jellies or Lemon Cheam.
5. A Hunter's Pudding.	5. Jellies.	5. Solomon Gandie.
6. Roafted Tongue.	6. A Hare or Woodcocks.	6. Cuftards.
7. A Ham or Roaft Beef.	Collar'd Beef.	7. Boil'd Turkey with Oyfter Sauce.
Remove. 1. Fifh.	8. CreamCurds.	Remove. 1. Wild Duck.
	9. Ducks or Pig.	

Elizabeth Moxon provided these table plans to enable her readers to place every dish in its correct position, between seven and nine dishes per course being quite usual on fashionable tables of the 1740s.

For the first course at dinner, the main midday meal, Elizabeth Moxon in the 1740s had set at the top of the table either a delicate stewed meat, a cooked fish, or a soup, the latter perhaps being removed once it had been served by the hostess, and replaced by a stewed meat. In the middle there might be a boiled pudding, a dish of pickles, shellfish, or a salad, while at the bottom lay a substantial joint of roast, boiled or stewed meat ready to be carved and served by the host. At the four corners there were savoury dishes of meat, fish or pudding, to complete the usual symmetrical arrangement of seven dishes, although there might be two more dishes, one to each side of the middle one, for a larger meal of nine dishes, or the two side dishes could replace the four corner dishes to make a smaller meal of five dishes. By the 1760s the fashion for arranging the first course at dinner had apparently changed, for Ann Peckham usually set fish at the top of the table and a dish of soup in the middle, but then followed the previous arrangement of a major roast or a pasty at the bottom, and the usual range of side and corner dishes.

For the second course at dinner, both authors placed stewed or roast game and poultry at the top and bottom of the table, with a dish of fresh or preserved fruit, or syllabubs, creams or jellies in glasses, in the middle, and a variety of the more delicate shellfish, game, fruit and pastries all around.

For supper, the second main meal of the day, served in the early evening, only one course was set on the table, with boiled, stewed or fried poultry, game, and the more delicate meats such as lamb set at the top and bottom, Elizabeth Moxon also including fish, and warming dishes of plumb gruel, rice gruel or sack possets for the cold winter months of the 1740s, although these were omitted by Ann Peckham in the 1760s. In the middle, there were fruits, creams and jellies, while the side and

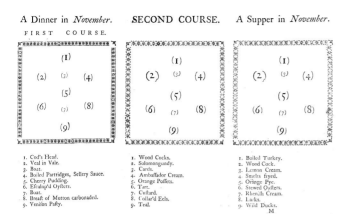

A Dinner in *November.*　　SECOND COURSE.　　A Supper in *November.*
FIRST   COURSE.

1. Cod's Head.
2. Veal in Vale.
3. Boat.
4. Boiled Partridges, Sellery Sauce.
5. Cherry Pudding.
6. Efcalop'd Oyfters.
7. Boat.
8. Breaſt of Mutton carbonaded.
9. Veniſon Paſty.

1. Wood Cocks.
2. Solomongundy.
3. Cards.
4. Ambaſſador Cream.
5. Orange Poſſets.
6. Tart.
7. Cuſtard.
8. Collar'd Eels.
9. Teal.

1. Boiled Turkey.
2. Wood Cock.
3. Lemon Cream.
4. Smelts fryed.
5. Orange Pye.
6. Stewed Oyſters.
7. Rheniſh Cream.
8. Larks.
9. Wild Ducks.

These plans show Ann Peckham's table plans of the 1760s. With a total of eighteen dishes at dinner served in the early afternoon, and a further nine at supper in the evening, the Leeds merchants certainly had ample choice at their formal dinners.

corner dishes included all manner of sweet and savoury delicacies.

The recreation of a completely authentic menu from the 18th century could be quite difficult and expensive, particularly if it was to include ingredients such as lobsters, oysters, lampreys, sucking pigs, calves' heads, veal, cod's heads, larks, thrushes or lapwings. However, the following series of recipes, all using the authentic methods and ingredients readily available today, will enable anyone to plan, cook and serve a dinner as if for a merchant of Georgian Leeds. The recipes are arranged in the order in which they would be set on the table in the 1760s, with a selection of top, bottom, side and corner dishes respectively:

First Course for Dinner: Top Dishes

Salmon in Cases[8]

6 salmon steaks	50g/2oz butter
15ml/1tbs fresh parsley	100g/4oz fresh white breadcrumbs
45ml/3tbs spring onions	juice of one lemon
45ml/3tbs mushrooms	salt and pepper
writing paper or cooking foil	

1. Skin the salmon.
2. Mix the very finely chopped parsley, spring onions and mushrooms with the butter, pepper and salt, and stir-fry them until cooked.
3. Remove the pan from the heat, take each steak in turn and lightly rub it in the butter and vegetables, then place it in a shallow case made from either folded writing paper or cooking foil.
4. When all the steaks have been put in their cases, cover them with the fried vegetables, sprinkle them with the breadcrumbs, and bake at 170°C, 325°F, gas mark 3 for 20-30 minutes, depending on the thickness of the fish.
4. Serve on a hot dish with a small boat of the lemon juice.

To Fry Trout[9]

6 cleaned trout	100g/4oz browned bread crumbs
1 large egg, beaten	75g/3oz butter

1. Wipe the fish clean with kitchen paper.
2. Brush them with the beaten egg on one side, dip in breadcrumbs, then repeat on the other sides, and fry them in the butter two at a time for 12-15 minutes, turning them once, then drain them with kitchen paper and place them on

a warm serving dish until all are ready to be served (herrings can also be cooked in this way, and served with thinly-sliced onions, fried light brown, and a boat of melted butter and mustard).

To boil herrings[10]

6 herrings, cleaned and washed	2 anchovy fillets
10ml/2tsp salt	30ml/2tbs fresh parsley
half a light stock cube	lemon slices
100g/4oz butter	sprigs of parsley for garnishing

1. Remove the milts and roes from the herrings.
2. Bend the herrings into as small a circle as possible, skewer in place, then tie them around with thin string.
3. Put the herrings, spine downwards, in a pan, with the milts and roes, just cover them with water, add the salt, bring them slowly to the boil, and cook for 7-10 minutes, until tender.
4. Meanwhile stew the parsley, drain it, chop it finely, place it into a pan with the anchovies and butter, and cook together until the anchovies have melted, then pour the mixture into a small bowl as a sauce.
5. Lift the fish out on a slice, turn them over, allow them to drain, arrange them around a dish, with the bowl of sauce in the middle, the milts and roes between each fish, and garnish with the lemon slices and sprigs of parsley.

First Course: Middle Dishes

To make Green Pease Soop[11]

450g/1lb fresh or frozen peas	30ml/2tbs rice
5ml/1tsp salt	1 small beetroot
6 peppercorns	1 slice of white bread
1 lamb stock cube	

1. Simmer the peas in 600ml, 1 pt water for 15 min if fresh, 5 min if frozen.
2. Drain the peas, retaining the liquid in a large saucepan.
3. Take out 50ml, 3tbs of the peas to use later, and rub the remainder through a nylon sieve, using the back of a spoon, to separate the pulp from the husks.
4. Place the sieve over the saucepan, and pour over 600ml/1pt water to rinse the husks.
5. Stir the pea pulp into the water in the saucepan, then adding the salt, peppercorns and the crumbled stock cube.
6. Bring 300ml/½pint water to the boil in a small pan, add the rice and a pinch of salt, and simmer for 15-20 minutes until tender, then drain and rinse.
7. Cut the bread into small diamonds and fry them in butter as croutons, slice the beetroot, and stamp it into small rounds.
8. Heat the soup to boiling, pour it into a deep dish, add the cooked peas and croutons, and decorate the rim with small piles of rice and the rounds of beetroot.

To make Hodge Podge[12]

675g/1½lb lean beef	15ml/1tbs mixed dried thyme,
100g/4oz lean ham	parsley, marjoram & a bayleaf
2.4l/4pt water	salt & pepper
225g/8oz turnips	2 beef stock cubes
225g/8oz onions	100g/4oz cooked green peas
225g/8oz carrots	

1. Cut the beef into large cubes, put them into a large pan with the crumbled stock cubes, and bring it to the boil.

2. Add the peeled and diced or scooped vegetables, the herbs, a little salt and pepper, and gently simmer them for some 1 hour 30 min to 2 hours until they are tender, and stir in the peas just before serving.

To make Almond Soup[13]

This is an interesting example of a soup which contains a large piece of meat, in this case a chicken. The soup can be ladled out into bowls, and the chicken then cut up and served separately.

1.4 kg/3lb oven-ready chicken	2 chicken stock cubes
125g/5oz flaked almonds	10ml/2tsp salt
3 hard-boiled egg yolks	1ml/¼tsp mace
1 sterilised egg white	red food colouring

1. Liquidise or blend the almonds, egg yolks and stock cubes with 450ml/¾pt of water, pour the milky liquid through a fine strainer into a large saucepan, returning the residue to the liquidised with more water until all the flavour has been extracted, then add sufficient water to the pan to make up to 2.4l/4pts.
2. Rub the chicken with the salt and mace, and place in the saucepan with the almond liquid, bring it to the boil, and simmer for about 50 minutes, until the chicken is tender.
3. Just before serving, beat the egg white to stiffness, as if making a meringue, and divide it into two, colour one half pink with the food colouring.
4. Put the chicken into a large dish, pour the soup around it, and decorate the edge of the dish with alternate spoonfuls of the pink and the white beaten egg.

First Course: Bottom Dishes

Roast Beef

Around 1.5kg, 3lb roasting joint of beef cooked at 130°C, 350°F, gas mark 4 for:

15 min per 450g/1lb plus	15 min for rare
20 min per 450g/1lb plus	20 min for medium
25 min per 450g/1lb plus	25 min for well done

To Stew a Rump of Beef[14]

about 1,5kg, 3lb silverside or brisket	5ml/1tsp peppercorns
a few slices of fat bacon	a bouquet garni.
60ml/4tbs chopped fresh parsley	25g/1oz butter
600ml/1 pt claret	30ml/2tbs flour
3 anchovy fillets	10ml/2tsp salt
1 onion,coarsely chopped	grated horseradish.
a blade of mace	1 cooked beetroot

1. Weigh the joint and calculate the cooking time at 30 min per 450g, 1lb, and 30 min over, up to around 1.5kg, 45 min per 450g, 1lb for larger joints.
2. Lard the joint with strips of the fat bacon and stuff it with the parsley, roll it up tightly and truss it with cotton tapes.
3. Place in a large pan with 1.8l/3 pt water, the claret, anchovies, onion, mace, peppercorns and bouquet garni, cover the pan, bring to the boil, skim it carefully, reduce the heat until just bubbling, and simmer until cooked.
4. Stain the liquor into a separate pan with the salt and thicken with the flour worked into the butter, stirring it to boiling point. Place the joint in a hot dish, pour the sauce round it, and garnish the rim of the dish with piles of horseradish and slices of beetroot.

Beef Pasty[15]

550g/1¼lb rump or sirloin steak	For the pastry:
50g/2oz sugar	300g/11oz plain flour
150ml/¼pt claret	75g/3oz butter
pinch of salt and pepper	1 egg white
1ml/¼tsp ground nutmeg	

1. Beat the meat flat with a rolling pin, rub the sugar into both sides and leave in a cool place for 24 hours.
2. Pour the claret over the meat, and sprinkle with the salt, pepper and nutmeg.
3. Rub a third of the butter into the flour, then stir in the egg white with just sufficient water to form a firm pastry, then roll this out into a strip some 130cm/5ins wide, put a third of the remaining butter on two-thirds of the length of pastry, fold it in three, and roll it out once more to the original size, repeating this twice with the remaining butter, then set it aside to chill for 30 minutes.
4. Roll the pastry into two large rectangles. Place one half either on a baking sheet, or in a shallow baking tin, place the meat inside, damp the edges, cover with the other piece of pastry, seal the edges, brush with milk, prick with a fork, and bake at 200°C, 400°oF, gas mark 6 for 30 min, then reduce to 180°C, 350°F, gas mark 4 for a further 45 minutes. Eat either hot or cold.

Pork Griskins & Apple Sauce[16]

6 pork loin steaks	3 medium cooking apples
5ml/1tsp each of salt, pepper and dried sage, mixed together	

1. Wipe and core the apples, place in a baking dish with a little water, and bake for 45-60 minutes at 200°C, 400°F, gas mark 6 until soft. Remove the pulp with a spoon and mash it with a fork to form the apple sauce [this may be sweetened to taste].
2. Lightly dust the steaks with the salt, pepper and sage, and cook them under a hot grill for 8-10 minutes each side.

First Course: Side & Corner Dishes

To Boil Fowls[17]

1.4kg/3lb oven-ready chicken	30ml/2tbs cream
10ml/2tsp salt	1ml/¼tsp ground mace
275ml/½pt milk	a few button mushrooms
50g/2oz fresh white breadcrumbs	

1. Place the chicken and salt in a large pan, just cover with the milk and water, bring to the boil, then reduce to a simmer for about 50 minutes.
2. Meanwhile stew the mushrooms in the butter, add the cream, mace and breadcrumbs, then stir in 275-425ml/½-¾pt of the chicken stock, and simmer a few minutes to make the sauce.
3. Drain the chicken, place on a hot dish, and cover with the sauce.

Beef Olives[18]

6 thin slices of steak [500g/20oz]	30ml/2tbs suet
75g/3oz fresh white breadcrumbs	3ml/½tsp parsley
3ml/½tsp salt	3ml/½tsp thyme.
1ml/¼tsp ground mace	1 beaten egg yolk
1 beaten egg	browned breadcrumbs
pinch black pepper	a little beef gravy

1. Make a forcemeat by mixing together the salt, herbs, spices, suet and fresh breadcrumbs with the whole beaten egg, and form it into six rolls.

2. Lightly beat out the steaks, roll each one round a piece of the forcemeat, brush it with the beaten egg yolk, roll in the brown breadcrumbs, and place in a greased baking dish.

3. Bake at 180°C, 350°F, gas mark 4 for 1 hour 15 minutes, then cut them in two longways, lay them on a hot serving dish, and serve with beef gravy.

Mutton Collops[19]

675g/1lb 8oz lean leg of mutton 1 onion, finely chopped
salt and pepper   225g/8oz butter
1ml/¼tsp ground mace   300ml/½pt lamb stock
15ml/1tbs fresh chopped parsley 100g/4oz mushrooms

1. Cut the lamb in very thin slices, put them into a saucepan with the salt and pepper, mace, parsley and chopped onion, and stir-fry with the butter for a few minutes until the meat is just cooked, then put them into a hot dish and keep them warm.

2. Stew the sliced mushrooms in the lamb stock for 5-10 min, pour them over the collops in the dish, and serve hot.

One of Elizabeth Moxon's 1741 dinners for about six people. Chosen for a first course for a dinner in April, it includes top, a fillet of veal, at the bottom, a roast leg of lamb, in the middle a hunter's pudding, and at the sides salt fish, and beefsteaks.

Hunter's Pudding[20]

225g/8oz plain flour   grated peel of one lemon
150g/6oz suet   1ml/¼tsp ground nutmeg
150ml/6oz currants   2ml/½tsp salt
50g/2oz raisins   2 eggs, beaten
50g/2oz sugar   150ml/¼pint cream
15ml/1tbs brandy
For the sauce: 450ml/¾pt white wine
30g/2oz sugar   30g/2oz butter

1. Mix together all the dry ingredients, make a well in the centre, pour in the cream, eggs and brandy, and stir together, adding sufficient water to form a soft mixture.

2. Rinse a large square of muslin, squeeze it dry, dust one side with a little flour, shake off the surplus, and place it over a basin, place the mixture in the cloth, fold the muslin over it, tie it securely, and plunge it into boiling water, and continue boiling for three hours.

3. Make the sauce by melting the ingredients together, and heating them almost to boiling. When the pudding is ready, drain it, quickly dip it in cold water, drain it, turn it out on to a plate, and serve with a boat full of the sauce.

Second Course: Top Dishes

Roast Chicken

2.3kg/5lb oven-ready chicken, roasted at 200°C, 400°F, gas mark 6, for 2 hours, basting occasionally.
For the sauces, chicken gravy to go into the serving dish, and 30ml/2tbs finely chopped parsley slowly stewed in 150g/6oz butter.

How to make a Brown Fricasey of Chickens[21]

900g/2lb chicken breasts or thighs 5ml/1tsp salt
100g/2oz butter   15ml/1tbs flour
450ml/¾pt chicken stock   25g/1oz butter
45ml/3tbs white wine   1 slice white bread
1ml/¼tsp grated nutmeg   sprigs of parsley

1. Cut the chicken into pieces suitable for eating, and fry them for about two minutes until light brown in the butter.

2. Add the chicken stock, wine, nutmeg and salt, and simmer very gently for about an hour.

3. Cut the bread into small diamonds or triangles, and fry them as croutons.

4. Work the butter into the flour, add it to the chicken stock, and stir until it thickens, then pour it into a hot dish, and garnish the rim with the croutons and the parsley.

To Roast Moor-Game

6 oven-ready grouse, roasted at 200°C, 400°F, gas mark 6, for 40 minutes
For the bread sauce: 75g/3oz fresh white breadcrumbs
     1 medium onion
     450ml/¾pt milk
     4 cloves
     salt and pepper

1. Stick the cloves into the onion, put into a pan with the milk, bring to the boil, remove from the heat, and leave to infuse for 10 minutes.

2. Stir in the bread, cook gently, stirring gently for a few minutes until it thickens, then remove the onion, add salt and pepper to taste, and pour into a boat to serve with the grouse.

Second Course: Middle Dishes

To make Calf's Foot Jelly[22]

20ml/4tsp gelatin   15ml/1tsp brandy
300ml/½pt water   juice of one lemon
300ml/½pt white wine   30ml/2tbs sugar

1. Filter the lemon juice through a coffee filter paper, pouring it through twice.

2. Bring the water to the boil. Sprinkle the gelatin into half the white wine, and immediately pour on the boiling water, stir until it has dissolved, then stir in all the remaining ingredients, including the filtered lemon juice, then pour into small wineglasses and place in a cool place to set.

Ribbon Jelly[23]

1. *Using either food colouring or fruit syrups, divide the above jelly into six portions and colour separately as cochineal red, green, saffron yellow, purple [originally syrup of violets], white [with a little cream], and clear.*
2. *Pour 1cm/½inch layers, of the jelly into tall narrow glasses, leaving each one to set before the next is poured in, contrasting the colours to give an attractive appearance.*

To make White Lemon Cream[24]

450ml/1pt water	15ml/1tbs orange flower water
6 whites of free-range eggs	juice of 3 lemons
225g/8oz sugar	

1. *Beat the egg whites in a large bowl, to just break them together, then add the remaining ingredients, mix together until the sugar has dissolved, then strain the liquid through a cloth into a saucepan.*
2. *Heat the liquid gently, slowly stirring, and skimming off any froth, until it just starts to thicken, as if making a custard, for it would quickly curdle if it approached boiling point, then pour into six wineglasses, and leave to cool, when it will partly set.*

Second Course: Bottom dishes

To Roast Ducks[25]

1 oven-ready duck	salt and pepper
1 onion, finely chopped	50g/2oz butter
5ml/1tsp dried sage	

1. *Rub the inside of the duck with a little salt and pepper, mix together the onion, sage and butter, put this inside the duck, then roast it at 200°C, 400°F, gas mark 6 for 20 minutes per 450g/1lb, plus 20 minutes.*

Roast Turkey

1 oven-ready turkey, about 2.3kg/5lb, roasted at 180°C, 350°F, gas mark 4, calculating the cooking time as in the previous recipe.

Second Course: Side and Corner Dishes

To boil Asparagus[26]

Scrape all the stalks carefully, till they look white, cut them even [in length] and tie them in little bunches, put them in a pan of boiling water and salt, and let them boil gently [12-15 minutes], till they are tender, then take them up: make a toast, lay it on the dish, and pour a little butter over it: lay the asparagus all round the dish, with the heads in the middle, and serve it with butter in a boat.

To boil Carrots

Wash and boil them, and when enough, peel off the out-side, slice them on to a plate, and serve them with butter in a boat, young carrots will take half an hour in boiling: if larger they will take an hour.

To boil Cauliflowers

Take off the green part, and either cut them in quarters or boil them whole, lay them an hour in water, then boil them in milk and water, skimming it well: when the stalks are tender, take them carefully up to drain, and serve them up with butter in a boat.

To stew Cucumbers

1 cucumber	15ml/1tbs salt
15ml/1tbs vinegar	600ml/1pt water
6 peppercorns	25g/1oz butter
1 light stock cube	15ml/1tbs flour

1. *Slice the cucumbers a quarter of an inch thick, and soak them for two hours in a brine made with the salt and water.*
2. *Drain the cucumbers, discard the brine, and add the vinegar, peppercorns, stock cube, and 600ml/1pt of water, and simmer for 10 minutes until just tender, then stir in the butter worked into the flour to thicken the liquid. The serving dish may be garnished with sippets of fried bread.*

To stew Pease

450g/1lb peas	1 coss lettuce, chopped small
2 small whole onions	25g/1oz butter
salt and pepper	15ml/1tbs flour
1 light stock cube	450ml/¾pt water

1. *Put the peas, onions and lettuce into a saucepan, cover, and cook gently to sweat for 10 minutes.*
2. *Add the water, salt and pepper, stock cube, and the flour worked into the butter, and shake uncovered over a medium heat until the peas are cooked and the sauce has thickened.*

As for the lesser meals of the day, breakfast was probably set out like this:[27]

Tea Table
Spread Bread & Butter
Seed Cake
Cold Capon
Chocolate
Cold Pots
Cheesecakes
Sliced Tongue & Butter
Ham of Bacon

The tea table also enjoyed regular use at other times of the day, especially in the afternoon and in the drawing room after dinner. The tea itself was available in many varieties from the specialist dealers in the town, of whom there were 13 by 1798. Chinese green and bohea (the finest kind of black tea made from the first buds of the new crops) were the most popular types. Supplies sometimes came in from smugglers, but, as the *Leeds Intelligencer* of 15 April 1777 reported, this could bring the unwelcome attention of the revenue men: "A person in Pudsey bought some run goods at Hunmanby: on his return home, hearing some officers about Leeds were in pursuit of him, sent for the officer to his own house, and delivered up to him 66 pounds of black tea."

As for the tea equippage, the best teapots, jugs and basins were either of silver, or of imported china, such as that offered by auction at the Red Bear in Briggate in April 1777:[28] "Foreign China …large quantity of Table and Tea Services of China, both blue and white, Nankeen and coloured, likewise a very elegant assortment of Bamboo tables, Waiters, etc., …and some real Indian Soys". Around the middle of the 18th century "a kind of delftware …very creditable copies of Oriental patterns, with salt glaze" pottery was being made in Holbeck, but the real expansion of this trade took place with the founding of the Leeds Pottery around 1770.[29] Although both red stonewares and Egyptian blackwares were made here, the most important

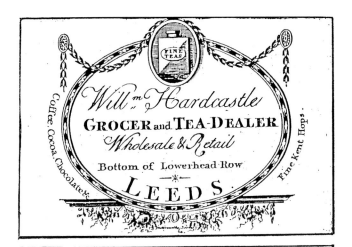

Leeds had a number of shopkeepers who specialised in selling teas, coffees and drinking chocolates. Both Thomas Smith and William Hardcastle, whose wife Hannah concentrated on the tea business, were trading in the town around 1800.

When Adam Baynes built Knostrop Hall in the mid-17th century, he included a fine banqueting house where he and his friends could enjoy fruit, sweetmeats and wines in a delightful garden setting. In the early nineteenth century, it was a popular tea garden where visitors took refreshments and were entertained by glee singers.

product was their finely-made cream-coloured earthenware, called Queensware. They made every imaginable article of tableware, both for use at dinner, where it replaced the earlier pewter services, and for the service and drinking of tea, coffee and chocolate, every piece being made to the most elegant design, and either left plain, or enriched with transfer-printed or brightly-coloured enamel decoration. These would be available for sale in the town, where in 1784 people such as John Dixon were trading as "China-man & Tea dealer" in Briggate, conveniently selling both products from the same shop.

Tea was not only taken in the home, for by the early 19th century tea gardens had been set up as very popular places of fashionable resort. One at Knostop Hall occupied a romantic 17th century mansion set on the banks of the Aire a couple of miles downstream from the town centre where around 1816 visitors could enjoy "Tea, Harrogate water, Ginger Beer, Cheese Cakes, etc." in gardens which still retained antique stone seats and a fine early banqueting house enriched with period statuary.[30] Here customers could arrive by barge, accompanied by a military band, and enjoy their tea while listening to the glee singers perform "Here in the Cool Grot and Mossy Cell". A similar establishment lay on the hills beyond the present Westgate roundabout, which offered delightful views over the still rural gardens, orchards and fields of the Aire valley, across to the woods of Middleton. Known as St Peter's Wood, or North Hall Gardens, it received the good folk of Leeds on afternoons, particularly Sundays, to drink tea, buy bunches of flowers and

flirt, or rather cout, for young men meant business in those days of the 1820s.[31]

Tea, coffee and chocolate would also have been drunk both in the Leeds Coffee House and in the supper room at the Assembly Rooms, the magnificent apartments built in 1776-7 above the White Cloth Hall for all the balls, concerts and other entertainments enjoyed by the Leeds merchants. This was the scene of the town's most exclusive entertainments and lavish catering, some impression of the grandeur of these functions being given in descriptions such as this report of the Yorkshire Archers Ball held on 26 October 1790:[32] "The company consisted of two hundred ladies and gentlemen of the first rank and fashion in the country. The Ladies appeared in white, with green ornaments, and afforded the greatest display of taste and elegance. The ball was opened at nine o'clock by a minuet danced by the Earl Fitzwilliam and the Countess of Mex-

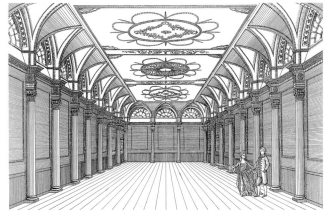

The ballroom at the Leeds Assembly rooms of 1776-7. This was the centre of the town's glittering social life, being used for balls, assemblies and concerts, during which magnificent refreshments were served in the adjacent supper rooms. Later it became the first Leeds Working Mens' Institute.

borough …Country dances commenced at ten, and the supper room was opened at 12 o'clock. It would be impossible to describe the decorations of the table …the propriety and brilliance with which they were ornamented reflect the highest credit on Mr Vickers of York. The effects of festoons of coloured lamps was particularly pleasing. Dancing continued till three o'clock in the morning, soon after which the company began to retire highly gratified with their evening's entertainment."

In the 1790s the flourishing state of Leeds' national and international cloth trade brought unprecedented wealth, much of which was devoted to the arts of good living. Two hundred years later we are experiencing an almost identical situation as the city's legal, financial and commercial success fosters the growth of new restaurants, health clubs, fine shops, and a lively nightclub scene.

Notes:

1. Borthwick Institute of Historical Research, York
2. quoted in M. Beresford, "East End, West End", *Thoresby Society,* LX & LXI, Leeds (1988) 163-4
3. M. Beresford, *Walks Around Red Brick*, Leeds (1980) 80
4. *ibid.,* 30 & 39-41
5. V. Maclean, *A Short-title Catalogue of Household and Cookery Books Printed in the English Tongue 1701-1800,* (1981)104-6
6. "Registers of the Leeds Chapelries", *Thoresby Society,* XXIII, Leeds (1915-16) & XXIX (1922)
7. G. Drury, *Chronicles of Families Connected to Kirkstall Forge,* (Typescript) I, 166
8. A. Peckham, *op.cit.,* 16
9. *ibid.,* 30 & 33
10. E. Moxon, *op.cit.,* 113
11. *ibid.,* 7
12. A. Peckham, *op.cit.,* 13
13. *ibid.,* 9
14. E. Moxon, *op.cit.,* 11
15. A. Peckham, *op.cit.,* 107
16. *ibid.,* 55
17. *ibid.,* 61
18. *ibid.,* 38
19. *ibid.,* 44
20. E. Moxon, *op.cit.,* 21
21. *ibid.,* 37
22. A. Peckham, *op.cit.,* 168
23. *ibid.,* 168
24. *ibid.,* 161
25. *ibid.,* 65
26. *ibid.,* 128-9 & E. Moxon, *op.cit.,* 151
27. Lord Hawkesbury, "Memorandum Book of a Yorkshire Lady", *East Riding Antiquarian Society,* 30
28. *Leeds Mercury,* 8/4/1777
29. H. Lawrence, *Yorkshire Pots and Potteries,* Wakefield (1974)61 & D. Towner, *The Leeds Potteries,* (1963)
30. *Leeds Mercury,* 27/7/1816
31. *Local Notes & Queries,* no.477
32. P. Brears, "The Leeds Assembly Rooms", *Georgian Group Journal,* (1994) 76-80

INDUSTRY & POVERTY

AS THE ever-increasing volume of trade demanded higher levels of productivity, more efficient wool and flax machinery was developed, and the entrepreneurs soon realised that these worked most efficiently when gathered together in centralised buildings. In 1791-92 John Marshall therefore built the world's first mechanical flax-spinning factory on Water Lane, Holbeck, while in 1797 Benjamin Gott began to create the world's first comprehensive woollen mill at Bean Ing on Wellington Street.[1] At first the weaving of linen and woollen cloths and the delicate finishing processes, etc., were still carried out by the traditional hand processes, but gradually these too were mechanised, effectively bringing the domestic system of production to an end around the 1860s. To enable these changes to take place, Leeds developed an amazingly versatile and innovative engineering industry, which produced the specialised machinery, the steam engines to power it, the locomotives to bring in the raw materials and carry away the finished goods, and the winding engines, etc., which enabled the local collieries to produce all the coal necessary to fuel the whole massive complex.

The social changes brought about by industrialisation were truly enormous, particularly as the new factories brought in a huge workforce. In the 1770s Leeds had a population of some 30,000. By the 1840s this had increased five-fold to around 152,000, tripling again to around 429,000 by 1900. This brought huge housing problems, particularly since the built-up area of Leeds in the 1770s was still constrained within its 13th century boundaries. The narrow garden plots behind the Briggate, Vicar Lane and Kirkgate frontages were now lined with rows of warehouse, shop and cottage properties, with paved communal yards in front, and blank walls behind, where they backed on to the next yard, as may be seen in the cottages of around 1790 in Turk's Head Yard off Briggate. When the town began to expand into the adjoining fields, especially to the east, thousands of similar houses were built in back-to-back rows, a system which made the maximum use of every scrap of available land.[2]

The first generation of back-to-backs were so closely packed together, with poor ventilation, no water supply, and the most primitive methods of sanitation that they rapidly degenerated into slums, especially during the 1840s influx of numerous poor families from Ireland, Scotland and various parts of rural England, who left their lives of agricultural poverty and near starvation to obtain work in the new factories. It was a situation virtually identical to that experienced in modern third-world countries, experiencing all the accompanying squalor, overcrowding, poor diet, death and disease. In the worst areas, the undrained, unpaved streets became a mass of liquid filth and excrement, through which numerous pigs enjoyed free range as they searched for food. The houses themselves, usually two or three storeys high, above a cellar, were frequently divided into separate one-room tenements, the poorest occupying the cellar area, which was entered by steps leading down from the street. One visited by Angus Reach in 1849 measured only seven feet (2m) square.[3] Its floor was littered with old bagging, Russian mats, old ropes and shavings, amid which stood rickety deal tables, two or three chairs more or less dilapidated, and a

bedspread on a small frame rolled up in one corner. The cooking apparatus consisted of a single pot.

About the same time Robert Baker asked s group of Leeds factory children how often they had meat. "We never get it," one answered, while another had it "sometimes once a week". "What then do you live upon?" "Coffee and bread or tea," came the reply.[4] For many workers, this was the standard diet for most of their lives. Even in the 1890s R. H. Sheracy was able to describe a visit to "one of the lowest neighbourhoods of Leeds, where I found an old slipper-maker at his tea. Although it was past ten at night, his five little children were with him. As his wife explained, "They've got to be there, when there's something to eat going. Father chucks them a bit of bread now and again, and they like to be there."[5] This was certainly the case in the 1890s in the tailoring industry, when one girl working in a sweat-shop recalled how she had "often been so weak for want of food that she had fainted over her machine. Many of her fellow workers used to beg food off the men in the factory, but she never cared to do this, as it led to things …When they were all very hungry, the foreman told them there were four hundred sailor suits coming up, would they do them at threepence [1p] each? They refused, as the lowst price was threepence halfpenny. The foreman kept them waiting a day and a half [without pay] and at last they were so hungry that they gave in."[6] In many households it was only the coming of wartime rationing that eventually enabled them to receive an adequate and balanced diet, even though it was still extremely sparse.

This drawing from Robert Sheracy's article on "The White Slaves of England" shows a Leeds slipper-maker's living room in the 1890s. Although his wife baked their bread, the whole family lived on bread and tea, with three-pennyworth of meat some weeks, and plenty of "working-man's beef" – onions.

The mainly bread and coffee diet of the poorer workers was certainly convenient, since the ingredients were easily bought from the shops and required the minimum of fuel and trouble to prepare, but it had nothing else to commend it. It was totally inadequate, and left them subject to illness and disease, so that by the end of the 19th century the workers' life expectancy dropped as low as 19 years, compared to 27 years for manufacturing tradesmen and shopkeepers, and 44 years for the gentry etc.[7] This level of poverty, together with the fact that many mothers now worked in the factories, and generations of children had to start earning as soon as they were able, instead of picking up domestic skills around the home, meant that many working families lost all knowledge of the economical yet very wholesome traditional diets and lifestyles they had followed before industrialisation.

One very simple recipe has survived from this period. It was obviously designed to make the best of any small pieces of cooked meat and fish, and could produce a quick and filling dish using only a frying pan:

Poverty Cakes

1 egg	*2.5ml/½tsp baking powder*
275ml/½pt milk	*225g/8oz flour*
pinch of salt	*fat for frying*
a few scraps of meat or fish.	

1. Sift the flour, salt and baking powder into a bowl, make a well in the centre, break in the egg, then mix in just sufficient milk, little by little, to form a soft dough.

2. Turn the dough out on to a floured board, knead in the meat, roll out 5mm/¼in thickness, cut into squares, and fry gently on both sides until puffed and golden brown.

These would provide a little comfort in those dark days in those industrial Leeds households where:[8]

> T'owd taaty chest is empty, an
> We've nearly done wer coils
> They'll bring us nah noa seck o'flour,
> Ner hardlins lewk this way,
> An' t'bit we've left al barely fit
> Another baakin' day
> Ah've just nah cum fra' t'butcher's shop:
> He showed a sullen face
> Net e'en a jimmy wod he trust
> He wish'd ma aght o' place.

For about a quarter of the workforce, there was just about enough income to provide a good basic diet. In 1832 Humphrey Boyle costed this as follows for a man, his wife and their three children:[9]

21lb flour for bread @ 2s 6d	3s 9d
3lb 8oz flour for puddings @ 2s 8d	8d
eggs	2d
yeast	1½d
3lb 8oz of oatmeal	2s 2d
1lb treacle	3½d
1lb 8oz sugar	10½d
1½oz tea	5d

This reconstruction shows the Yorkshire range, the stone 'slapestone" sink, the scrubbed table, iron pans and numerous other features typical of the kitchen/living rooms occupied by most working families in mid-Victorian Leeds. Here all the meals were both prepared and eaten at the same table.

2oz coffee	5½ d
5lb meat @ 6d	2s 6d
vegetables at 1d per day	7d
salt, pepper, mustard, vinegar	2d
7pt beer @ 1½d	10½d
Total	**13s½ d** [65p]

This came out of a total budget of £1 0s 3d [£1.01]. By today's standards this diet would seem to be lacking both in quality and in variety, but it would give everyone a bowl of porridge and treacle for breakfast, a good supply of home-made bread, and sufficient meat, vegetables and puddings both for the main Sunday dinner and for the plainer dinners throughout the week. The Hunslet foundryman described in Richard Spencer's poem *T'Dinner Haar* was probably living just about this level:

Lizzie, thear'z t'foundry bell ringin,
Clear t'table an' spread t'cloth,
Thi fayther's cumin ower t'moor:
Get t'basins aght fer t'broth:
Poor fella, he leks weary, he
Can hardlins get along:
He said he'd heavy work on hand,
An he is noan sa strong …

His wife then tells him how:

T'doaf hes risen beautiful
As ivver ah did see,
Soa tha sal hev sum nice new cake
When tha cums hoam ta tea.
Ah've gotten tha sum watter-cress,
An' washed em nice an clean:
Ah've pick'd all t'bits o'grass awaay,
An' they lewk fresh an' green.

Even so, broth, bread and watercress hardly provides enough sustenance to carry out a hard day's work in the fierce heat of a foundry.

As the verses suggest, free food was collected from the surrounding countryside whenever possible. In spring the fresh young hawthorn shoots were nibbled by both adults and children, being known as "bread and cheese", while in early autumn whole families went out blackberrying along the hedgerows. The riverbanks and rough fields were also scoured to obtain all the nettles, dandelions and burdocks required for making drinks at home.[11] Local children also collected sorrel, which they knew as greensauce, or goose grass, to stock the "dilly-houses" or play houses they made beneath the elder bushes or similar places. They then ate both the leaves and stalks, appreciating their sharp refreshing flavour.[12] Herbs were gathered too, or were purchased from traders who hawked them around the streets. Their main purpose was to make herbal teas, chamomile and balm teas both being refreshing, pennyroyal and horehound teas had a good reputation for helping bronchial troubles, sage tea helped "the nerves and the blood" while marshmallow and peppermint were good for the digestion.[13] In south Leeds some ladies used to gather their own selection of herbs, boiling them in their kitchen set-pots to make "diet drinks" which they sold at sixpence a bottle. It was usually drunk in the autumn, while others made similar potions with nettles etc., every spring, to "clear the blood" after winter.

To provide free meat, a coal-riddle propped up on a stick over a few crumbs was used to catch sparrows for making sparrow pie. This was particularly associated with colliers, their shift-work giving them the daylight hours to work allotments and catch the sparrows when the weavers and engineers were still in the factories. In Churwell the colliers' houses in Primrose walk were locally known as "Sparrow Barracks", and they even had a song which told how their grandfathers never went hungry since they always had sparrow pie to fall back on. Cheap food was also obtained by keeping a few rabbits in the back-yard or garden, or by keeping an allotment on which to grow vegetables and perhaps some livestock too. In Holbeck, for example, "Owd Robin t'Gardener" had a plot where:[14]

There's a shed for poultry, an
A little bit beyond,
Ya' ma' see a lot o' yolla ducks
Ar glidin' ower a pond.
An' he's a bonny pig i' t'sty,
He kills wun ivvery year,
An' that's a thing that helps him much
Three t'winter season drear…

It would be a great mistake to believe that all the working families in Leeds lived in the poor conditions and meagre diets described above. It is true that although the corporation began to demolish the worst of the properties in the 1870s, many of them were still occupied up to the 1930s, when they were replaced by the Middleton and other estates in the suburbs, and the huge Quarry Hill Flats in the city centre. From the opening years of the 19th century, however, there had always been well-built, well-designed houses available for the more prosperous working families. The town's factories, shops and offices offered excellent opportunities for making a decent income, and maintaining a good standard of living, especially when the husband, his wife and children were all in regular work. For families such as these there were good through-terrace houses, with small iron-railed front gardens and walled-in back yards. The later back-to-backs were also extremely well-built and convenient, with ample cellar-space for coal, washing and storage, large living rooms, narrow sculleries, and at least two bedrooms.[15] By 1918 almost threequarters of all Leeds households lived in back-to-back houses of this kind, and they still form a significant and popular section of the city's housing stock.

Where a scullery was provided, it usually housed a tap, a large fireclay sink, a set-pot boiler with its own coal-burning grate, a small table, wall-mounted shelves, and a door leading to the cellar steps, down to the keeping cellar, with its stone-topped table, and the coal-hole. The scullery was where most of the food preparation took place, but in houses without such a room, this work was carried out both at a dresser and sink on the window side of the kitchen/living room, and on its large square kitchen/dining table, its scrubbed top being covered with a tablecloth for family meals.

Although in later years a gas ring was often placed on top of the old set pot, virtually all the cooking was carried out on a large Yorkshire range in the living room. Probably made in one of the local foundries, such as Kirkstall Forge, or Nelson's, etc., this black-leaded cast iron range, with its fine mouldings and polished steel fittings, provided the major source of heat for the entire house. Once stoked up, its central grate provided radiant heat for toasting, for warming the room, for drying clothes, and for creating a wonderfully cosy atmosphere for those who bathed in the tin bath set on the clipped hearth rug, screened by the clothes horse on cold winter evenings. The top bar of the range, and perhaps a "falling crow" which hinged down from

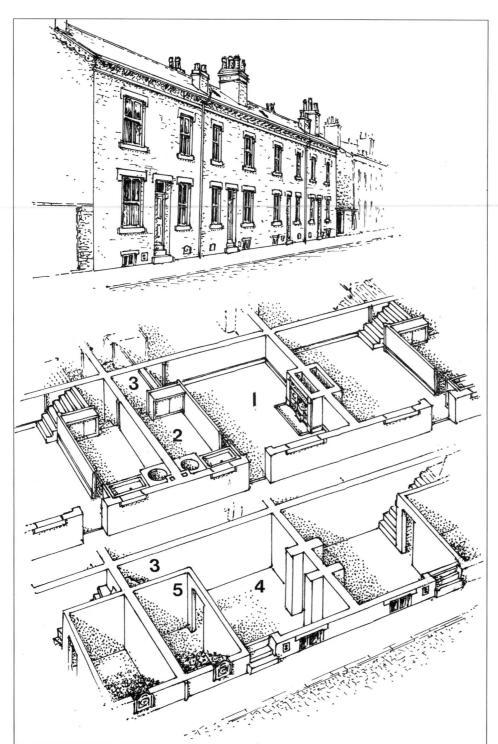

William Street, Headingley, is typical of thousands of back-to-back houses built around the city in the 1890s. It comprises;

Ground Floor
1. Kitchen/living room with Yorkshire range
2. Scullery, with sink, set pot and cupboard
3. Cellar steps

Cellar
3. Cellar steps
4. Keeping/storage cellar cupboard
5. Coal cellar with coal-hole from the street

Mrs G.Metcalf standing proudly in front of her fine Yorkshire range at Gledhow Walk, Burley, in 1981. Keeping the range in such splendid condition was a matter of real pride, for it took a great deal of time, trouble and elbow-grease to blacklead the ironwork, polish the bright fittings, the "tidy Betty" which covered the ash-pit, and the pierced brass "corners' which masked the angle between the range and the coloured enamel hearthplate.

the side of the oven, provided firm standings for iron pans for boiling vegetables and puddings, and kettles for boiling water. Over the top of the grate a large shelf was used for keeping warm the plates, dishes and teapots, and perhaps drying out the bundles of firewood used to kindle the fire. Within one hob there might be a side boiler, with a brass tap to run off the hot water, or there might be a fireback-boiler to supply a hot water system. Above the other hob, meanwhile, was a large cast-iron oven, with thick sheet-iron oven-plates, which could bake all manner of bread, puddings and cakes to perfection, once the housewife had mastered all its particular idiosyncrasies, and brought it firmly under her control.

For many families home baking presented real problems, since it required a great deal of time and energy. For this reason, many small bakers' shops were set up in the suburbs, each of them making all the breads, cakes, cooked meats, etc., which a family could want. Usually their standards were very high, so that even today the best still enjoy a flourishing trade, successfully beating off the competition provided by the supermarkets, and supplying fresh-baked oven cakes, loaves, and local specialities such as curd tarts, parkins, and cooked ham, etc., to their loyal and appreciative customers.

Even so, to many Victorian and Edwardian housewives the appearance of bought bread in the house was a matter of considerable shame, since it was only purchased by "those too idle to bake", and were not prepared to safeguard their families from the pernicious effects of the adulteration frequently practised at that time.[16]

In the home, the oatcake tradition of the handloom weavers had included large, flat loaves of white yeast-risen wheaten bread some nine inches (22cm) in diameter by about an inch and a half (4cm) in thickness, with a central dimple to stop them rising too much. To make the dough:[17]

> We'll fetch up that big yolla bowl,
> An ah'll leearn tha ta neyd up ta t'mark
> Soa, lass, tha ma roll up thi sleeves,
> Fer tha'll fin' at it's noa easy wark …
> There'z summat i' t'neydin, tha naws,
> An hevin thi oven i'trim:
> It's a job at wants watchin reight weel,
> An ne'er let thi fire get ta dim.

Having risen before the fire, they were baked on the stone or iron baxton hung over the glowing coals, first on one side and then on the other, to produce a fine browned crust on both sides. By the 1860s they were being baked on an oven-shelf set over the fire, but still retained their name of baxton cakes.[18] It was soon realised that it was much easier to cook them on the floor of the oven, and so they became the oven-bottom cakes which are still made and enjoyed in Leeds today. Fresh from the oven, they were often placed on the window-ledge or doorstep to cool, one then perhaps being split open, butter spread across its warm interior, and immediately eaten, the flavour of the fresh bread, its fine texture and soft crust and the succulence of the melted butter making it a greatly prized delicacy, even if it could cause chronic heartburn!

Oven Bottom Cakes

675g/1lb 8oz plain flour	10ml/2tsp sugar
5ml/1tsp salt	450ml/¾pt warm water
12g/½oz fresh yeast	100g/4oz lard at room temp
(or equivalent dried yeast)	

1. Sift the four and salt into a large bowl and make a well in the centre.
2. Dissolve the yeast and sugar in a little of the water (or activate the dried yeast according to the manufacturer's instructions).
3. Pour the yeast and water into the flour, mix it in and form into a soft dough. Turn this out on to a floured board and knead for 10 minutes, then return it to the bowl, cover it lightly, and leave in a warm place until doubled in size.
4. Cut the lard in small pieces and knead them into the dough, then form the dough into two large, or four small round, flat cakes, poke a deep hole in the centre of each with the finger, place them on a greased baking sheet, cover them once more, and leave to rise in a warm place until doubled in size once more.
5. Pre-heat the oven to 220°C, 425°F, gas mark 7, put in the oven cakes when ready, bake for 10 min, then reduce the temperature to 190°C, 375°F, gas mark 5 for a further 35 minutes.

Oven botton cakes were excellent for making ham and other sandwiches, for eating with cheese, and for being sliced and spread either with jam or with the delicious rich dark brown jelly and fat which settled at the bottom of bowls of beef dripping. The name "mucky fat" might not sound very appealing, but to connoisseurs of such matters it was a highly-regarded treat. A slice of oven-bottom cake was also ideal for mopping up the juices left in the frying pan after cooking a full breakfast. Those who went to Old Mother Sherwin's cookshop in Lands Lane around the 1850s could buy hot steaks enclosed in oven cakes which had been dipped in the red gravy, these being known by the descriptive name of "skull-draggers".[19] When broth containing pieces of meat was being served it was customary to break pieces of bread into it, these being known as sops, the served portion being describes as a "few" broth before the bread went in, and a "sop" of broth afterwards. The same distinction was made when serving boiled milk, or bread-and-milk, a common dish in Victorian Leeds.[20]

In order to cut down the rising time, and to avoid the indigestion caused by eating new bread, Goodall and Backhouse recommended replacing the yeast with baking powder to produce rather more scone-like Yorkshire teacakes:[21]

Yorkshire Teacakes

450g/1lb plain flour	15ml/3tsp baking powder
12ml/½tsp salt	300ml/½pt milk
25g/1oz butter	

1. Pre-heat the oven to 170°C, 320°F, gas mark 3.
2. Sift together the flour, salt and baking powder into a bowl and make a well in the centre.
3. Gently warm the butter with the milk until it has just melted, then leave it to cool for about 5 minutes.
4. Pour the milk into the flour etc., quickly mix it together to form a dough, knead it lightly and form it into four round flat cakes about 8-10cm/3-4ins in diameter.
5. Place on a greased baking sheet, and bake for around 30 minutes.

There were also a number of breads which could be made much more quickly, either in an emergency, when only a little flour was available, or to use up ingredients after a major baking session. These included flat cakes of flour kneaded with lard or dripping oven-baked for breakfast or tea, being so rich that they need not be buttered. Sad cakes were similar, being kneaded with dripping and baked in a frying pan, while short cakes were kneaded with either butter or with best dripping for Sundays, these being considered a great delicacy among the poor. There were also cracklin' cakes, small wheaten cakes pricked full of holes and baked so hard that they had to be soaked like a ship's biscuit before they were soft enough to eat.[22]

Pastries were popular too, including rhubarb tarts and apple pies, the latter always eaten with cheese, since as everyone knew, "an apple pie without the cheese is like the kiss without the squeeze". Then there were the currant pasties and mint pasties, the town of Yeadon being known locally as "Pastyland", for, it was claimed, the pasties made there were so big that while one end was in the oven, the other had to be propped up on the back of a chair in the middle of the room!

Mint Pasty

225g/8oz plain flour	30ml/2tbs finely chopped mint
2.5ml/½tsp salt	75g/3oz currants
100g/4oz butter, or half	50g/2oz sugar
butter, half lard	50g/2oz butter
about 45ml/3tbs water	

1. Preheat the oven to 200°C, 400°F, gas mark 6.
2. Sift together the flour and the salt, rub in the 100g/4oz of fat, stir in the water with a round-bladed knife, and lightly work to form shortcrust pastry.
3. Work the mint, currants and sugar in a bowl with the back of a spoon to make a uniform mixture.

4. Roll out the pastry into a large rectangle, spread the mixture thickly over one half, leaving a narrow margin around the edges, wet the edges, fold over the plain end of the pastry, then seal and trim the edges.

5. Pierce the upper crust in a few places with a fork, brush the pastry with a little milk or water, lightly sprinkle it with sugar, and bake on a greased baking sheet for 15 minutes.

There were cakes too, such as Jordan cake, remembered for being baked in the oven just after the joint had come out, and representing the only sweet cake of the week. Others made feather cakes, and also rich, crisp, light egg sponges.

For the regular meals throughout the week, breakfast often comprised white bread and treacle or bread and dripping washed down with cups of tap water or weak tea, bacon being reserved for Sunday mornings. The main meal, now served in the early evening, when everyone had returned either from work or from school, might be of stew, mince, pies, tinned meat with pickles and chips, rabbit, offal such as black pudding, liver and onions, or fried fish.[23] The menu for a typical Sunday dinner is provided in the following verse, which describes the food brought home to his wife and ragged children by a workman who, for the first time, had come directly home after being paid on Saturday night, rather than spending his wages in the Golden Fleece as usual:[24]

> Just lewk inta that henkitcher, [handkerchief]
> Ah've bowt five ribs o t'crop.
> A nicer bit o' meit Ah'm sewer
> Thear wern't i' t'butcher's shop
> Ah've bowt a peck o' nice green peys,
> Sum new potaaits az weel.
> Ah've bowt a carvin' knife an' fork,
> An a spankin' butcher's steel.

In some households nourishing mid-winter meals were prepared from sheeps' heads, some claiming that one of these could easily feed six people if properly dressed. First the head was split, soaked in salt water for two hours, cleaned, and then the brains scooped out into a muslin bag. The tongue was then removed, to be cooked separately and made into tongue sandwiches, and the eyes taken out, since they imparted a bitter taste. Some alleged that it was more economical to leave the eyes in, however, so that it could "see them through the week." The head was then placed in an iron saucepan with water, potatoes, pearl barley or lentils, the bag of brains being hung inside from a string tied to the pan handle, so that it would not touch the bottom and burn. After simmering on the hob, it was served hot, the brains being allowed to cool, and then eaten on toast.[25]

For vegetables to accompany the meat, there were of course all the potatoes, carrots, turnips, parsnips, cabbages, cauliflowers and peas, which were sold in the markets, or hawked around the streets. These were cooked as economically as possible, potatoes sometimes being put into a string bag and steamed, while peas were similarly put into bags, but then cooked in saucepans of boiling water, which was later drunk like soup. Split peas were used to make pease porridge and peas puddings, which were eaten with boiled meats[26]

Peas Pudding

225g/8oz split peas	*salt & pepper*
25g/1oz butter	*fresh breadcrumbs*

1. Soak the peas in water overnight, then tie the peas in a muslin cloth, and boil it for 2 hours.

2. Drain the peas, and either mash them or rub them through a sieve. Butter a pudding basin, sprinkle it with the breadcrumbs, press in the peas, and bake at 180°C, 350°F, gas mark 4 for 30 minutes and then turn out on to a plate.

Nettles also made a nourishing and freely-available vegetable, especially when the new growth had occurred in June. These were carefully picked, plunged into plenty of boiling water for ten minutes, drained, chopped and returned to the pan, and re-heated with a little pepper, salt and butter or cream just before serving.[27]

Boiled suet puddings continued to be as popular as ever, being simple to make, cheap, warming, and extremely satisfying. What were then known as blanket puddings, for their resemblance to a rolled blanket, or as a roll- or poke-pudding, we would now recognise as a jam rolly-poly, suet dough rolled into an oval, spread with jam, rolled up, tied in a pudding cloth, and then plunged into a pot of boiling water.[28] Here is another Leeds version:[29]

Apple & Currant Roly Poly

160g/6oz plain flour	*pinch of nutmeg*
75g/3oz suet	*50g/2oz currants*
2.5ml/½tsp baking powder	*225g/8oz peeled & cored apple*
2,5ml/½tsp salt	*75g/3oz sugar*

1. Cook the chopped apples with the sugar and 15ml/1tbs water in a covered pan, & when tender, mash them with a fork.

2. Mix the flour, suet, baking powder and salt together, and stir in just enough water to form a soft dough, roll it out, spread it with the apple puree, sprinkle with the currants and nutmeg, and roll it up.

3. Wrap the pudding in greased greaseproof paper, then in a cloth, tying the ends, put into a pan of rapidly boiling water, and boil for two hours. Serve with a sweet white sauce.

Although most of the food was probably bought from the shops and markets a substantial amount of seasonal food was hawked around the streets. Ann Scurr of Wortley recorded in

Many people earned their living by buying foods from the wholesalers and then selling them both around the streets and from door to door. These two women with their market baskets were shown at the busy junction of Boar Lane and Briggate in a view of Leeds on Market Day in 1872.

her diary for 5 August 1871 "First time this season I have noticed apples crying. Heard the crying of bilberries perhaps a fortnight ago", and on the 24th, "Field was crying potatoes yesterday at ¼d per score, that is more than they were at the fore-end of the week."[30] Other traders included the cockle-dealers crying "Cockles an' mussels eleyve, aw-al eleyve, Fine fresh cockles, Cockles an' mussels aw-al eleyve-oh!", or the pikelet girls, or the hot-cross bun dealers who carried their wares in wicker baskets covered with white cloths, and cried "Hot-cross buns, one-a-penny, two-a-penny, Hot cross buns!" Saturday night might also bring the spaw-water men, who carried a barrel hung with tin measures to serve out the reputedly medicinal waters from one of the local spas, such as those at Quarry Hill, Woodhouse, Weetwood, Potternewton or Armley Mills.[31] Perhaps the best-known street traders, however, were the cook-shop pie men. The contents of the pies were usually the subject of close and curious scrutiny:[32]

> So thar't a meat an' taty pie,
> Nay nivver that, its all mi eye,
> Bud come, fair play, ah will just try
> Ta fin' sum meit.
> It's true ther is sum thear, ah spy,
> Aw yes, its reight!
> If t'scraps o't dinner plates they've been
> It matters nowt, it can't be seen,
> Thear's no connectin' link between,
> An as fer t'gravy,
> Ta analize it 'ud puzzle e'en
> Sir Humphry Davy!

Sometimes they were honestly made of tripe, being known as trundle pies, but others were perhaps not too inaccurately surmised to contain plump pet pussy-cats. One customer after eating such a pie:[33]

> Inside he felt strange rumblings,
> And sounds to him quite new,
> And once or twice he could have sworn
> He heard a stifled mew!

To give flavour and piquancy to foods such as these, many bought a bottle of Goodall & Backhouse's Yorkshire Relish, which had developed from the home-made Yorkshire Dip of around 1800, and was still being made by Leeds housekeepers in the 1870s.[34]

Yorkshire Relish.

1.2l/2pt malt vinegar	*30ml/2tbs sugar*
2 English onions, chopped	*30ml/2tbs ground cloves*
30ml/2tbs black treacle	*5ml/1tsp chillies*

Simmer all the ingredients, except half the vinegar, in a stainless steel saucepan, until the onions are quite soft, then add the remaining vinegar, pour into sterilised bottles, and cork or screw down for use as required.

or[35]

Burnt Onions

225g/8oz onions	*300ml/½pt malt vinegar*
600ml/1pt water	*pinch of cayenne pepper*
225g/8oz brown sugar	

1. Bring the ninegar and cayenne almost to the boil, and allow it to cool.
2. Peel and finely chop the onions, put them in a saucepan with

the water, cook them together for five minutes, stir in the sugar, and continue stirring over a high heat until the onions turn dark brown and caramelise, then remove from the heat, carefully pour in the vinegar, little by little, still stirring, until it is cold, then bottle for use.

Of all the ready-cooked foods which were available to the working families of Victorian Leeds, the most popular by far were fish and chips. For a quick, hot, flavoursome, satisfying and economical meal they were unbeatable. Although fried fish had already been sold by some shops in Leeds, the first to sell both fish and chips was set up by a Londoner, Mr Edward Lewis, in Marsh Lane in 1880. This was so successful that he then started another at 131 West Street. His advertising handbill for

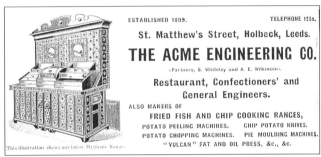

Founded as bicycle manufacturers, the Acme company soon became one of the country's leading and most innovative makers of equipment to the fish and chip trade. This beautiful tiled range was their latest design for 1904.

this venture announced "Excellent suppers of fried fish and chipped potatoes [à la mode de Paris] cooked in the best dripping and in a manner that private culinary art cannot compete with, may be had every evening from 6pm to 11pm. E. Lewis of London, who established the first fish and chip shop in Leeds, begs that "everyone will give this supper a trial."[36] From this time fish and chip shops sprang up in every part of the town, well over 300 flourishing here by 1900, most of them being in the suburbs. Henry Youngman could remember that the first hour of every evening was almost entirely for chips, both for factory hands nearby, and for children going to bed, a penny bag of chips being bought for each child, since there were always arguments if their parents tried to divide a larger quantity into individual portions at home.[37] The popularity of fish and chips continued undiminished, and there are still many local people who remember Fred Austin's song:

> Chips and Fish! Chips and Fish!
> Eh! by gum its a Champion Dish.
> Oh! what a smell when they fry 'em,
> Just get a penn'orth and try 'em.
> Put some Salt and Vinegar on, as much as ever you wish.
> You can do, do, do without supper, when you've
> Had a bob's worth o' Chips and Fish!

At first the frying was carried out in ordinary iron set-pots, but soon local engineering companies began to manufacture beautifully designed frying ranges. One of the major firms, Acme Engineering of Stocks Hill, Holbeck, had started manufacturing bicycles in 1879, but then moved on to potato peelers in 1899, and then abandoned bikes altogether to concentrate on their frying ranges. Other Leeds companies, such as Craven and Tattersall of Millshaw Works in Beeston, refined pure beef dripping specially for the fish-frying trade, while others produced the accompanying vinegar.

For those working in the centre of the town, and who could not return home for their meals, there were plenty of small cheap eating houses, and of course numerous pubs which provided both food and drink at reasonable prices. To provide a cheaper, non-alcoholic alternative, the first Leeds Working Men's Institute was set up in the Assembly Rooms in 1861. This was an immediate success, and was attracting some 1,800 to 2,000 men each week around 1865, when J. Tomlinson was shown around it by his friend Edwin:[38] "We must pay one penny each, whereby we can claim the privileges of membership for a week, so we betook ourselves first to a large and handsome reading room …In this room there were not less than 150 working men and youths, and, it being dinner time, a number of them were doing justice to sundry steaks, chops, and savoury rashers of bacon, the viands were supplied to them through a trap-door from the kitchen: the recipients paying one half-penny each for the cooking. No intoxicating drinks are allowed on the premises, but any of the members can have tea or coffee on payment of one penny per cup, and bread and butter or muffins at equally reasonable rates. Everyone seemed quite at home, laughing, chatting, eating, and evidently appreciated the advantages conferred by the institution … Afterwards we went into the wash-room, which is fitted up with every convenience, and where the working man may wash his hands and face, without any fee, before sitting down to eat or read. 'This is a capital institution,' said I, as we retired from the building, 'and almost sure to succeed.'"

Not only did it succeed, but within a few years similar facilities, although perhaps a little more up-market, were being set up to serve the growing demand for temperance establishments. These were the cocoa houses, such as Brussels Hall, Lockhart's, and the Leeds Public Cocoa Houses, which completed the working man's dining facilities in the town centre.

Notes:

1. S. Burt & K. Grady, *The Illustrated History of Leeds*, Derby (1994) 87-130
2. M. Beresford, "East End, West End", *Thoresby Society*, LX & LXI (1988) 202 *et.seq.*
3. A. B. Reach (C. Aspin, ed.) *The Yorkshire Textile District in 1849*, Helmshore (1974) 7
4. R. Baker, *Report on the Conditions of the Residence of the Labouring Classes in the Town of Leeds*, Leeds (1839) 45-6
5. R. Sheracy, "The White Slaves of England", *Pearson's Magazine*, II (1896) 263-8
6. *ibid.*
7. H. Whone, *The Essential Wast Riding*, East Ardsley (1975) 92
8. R. Spencer, *Field Flowers*, Batley, (1890)
9. W. G. Rimmer, "Working Men's Cottages in Leeds 1770-1840", *Thoresby Society*, CLVI (1963) 199
10. R. Sheracy, *op.cit.*, 346
11. *ibid.*, 276
12. Anon., *Dialect of Leeds*, (1862) 315
13. Yorkshire Archaeological Society MS 745
14. R. Spencer, *op.cit.*
15. L. Caffyn, *Worker's Housing in West Yorkshire 1750-1920*, (1986) 107-123
16. Anon., *Dialect of Leeds*, (1862) 256
17. R. Spencer, *op.cit.*, 326
18. Anon., *Dialect of Leeds*, (1862) 241
19. J. H. Wilkinson, *Leeds Dialect Glossary & Lore*, Leeds (1924) 12
20. Anon., *Dialect of Leeds*, (1862) 292
21. Goodall & Backhouse, *Good Things Made, Said & Done*, Leeds (1893) 78
22. Anon., *Dialect of Leeds*, (1862), 290, 296, 403 & 276
23. R. Hoggart, quoted in S. Burt & K. Grady, *op.cit.*, 215
24. R. Spencer, *op.cit.*, 320
25. Information from Yeadon Ladies Guild
26. A. Atkinson & G. Holroyd, *Practical Cookery*, Leeds (6th ed, 1911) 101
27. F. White, *Good Things in England*, (1932, 1974 ed.) 213
28. Anon., *Dialect of Leeds*, (1862) 251 & 394
29. A. Atkinson & G. Holroyd, *op.cit.*, 158
30. W. Benn, *Wortley-de-Leeds*, Stanningley (1926) 82
31. J. H. Wilkinson, *op.cit.*, 52 & 18
32. R. Spencer, *op.cit.*, 285
33. J. Hartley, *A Sheaf from the Moorland*, (1880) 175
34. Castle Museum, York. MS recipe book of Ellen Bulmer of St Mark's Villa, Leeds, 1878
35. *ibid.*
36. *Yorkshire Evening Post* 15/10/1984
37. *ibid.*, 5/11/1988
38. T. Tomlinson, *Some Interesting Yorkshire Scenes*, (1865) 25-6

LEARNING TO COOK

FOR centuries, most girls had learned their culinary skills from their mothers, starting to help around the kitchen when only a few years old. In this way they thoroughly absorbed all the traditional knowledge of cooking which they would require when setting up their own homes, and then pass it on to future generations. By this long and seemingly continuous process, a distinctively regional pattern of cookery had gradually evolved, one which made the most practical, wholesome and economical use of their resources. So long as the domestic textile industry flourished, all the traditional household skills continued as before, but then, from around the 1790s to the 1840s, the development of the factory system caused them to go into a period of rapid decline. Now both mothers and children spent most of their waking hours tending the steam-driven spinning machines, and later the power looms, in the large textile mills, only returning home for hurriedly-prepared meals and welcome sleep. After two or three generations, the decline in the quality of working-class home-life, and consequently the poor health of many Leeds families, had become very obvious to anyone prepared to take the trouble to notice it.

In late Victorian Britain, where the bible was widely read and discussed by all sections of society, the duties of the housewife were still seen in terms of Solomon's *Proverbs, Chapter 31*. Although she had only ceased to "seek wool and flax", lay "her hands to the spindle, and her hands hold the distaff" a few years before, after thousands of years of cloth production in the home, she was still expected to "bringeth her food, giveth meat to her household, …looketh well to the ways of her household, and eateth not the bread of idleness."[1] She could do few of these things, however, if she had neither the resources, nor the knowledge to supply the essentials of good housekeeping.

To remedy this situation, the wives of the leading Leeds industrialists, particularly Mrs Catherine Buckton and Mrs Emily Kitson, and a number of lady volunteers began a series of winter lectures on physiology and hygiene for working women in 1871.[2] It soon became obvious that their efforts were totally inadequate to undertake such an enormous task, however, and so they began to promote a number of new policies. In 1874 the Yorkshire Ladies' Council of Education used funds raised by subscription to open the Leeds School of Cookery in Cookridge Street. Both Mrs Titus Salt of the famous textile family which founded Saltaire, and Mrs Kitchen drew up a detailed syllabus to ensure that the wives of working men would be able to identify the healthiest foodstuffs, and the most nutritive and economical way of preparing them. They also recognised that it was extremely important that all the girls in the elementary schools should be taught how to cook.

At first the School provided lessons of two kinds. At 3.30pm well-to-do ladies and their cooks paid 6d [2.5p] each for tuition in "high-class", "middle-class", or "superior" cookery, their subscriptions helping to subsidise the "women of the industrial class" who paid 1d (½p) each for their classes at 8pm, by which time they had hopefully completed their day's work, fed their families, and finished their housework. This scheme proved extremely successful, and so it was possible to move to permanent accommodation in Upper Albion Street, where

Baroness Burdett-Coutts opened the Yorkshire Training School of Cookery, Leeds Branch, in 1875. In addition to their existing courses, the School was soon offering recognised qualifications both in domestic economy, in cookery, and in teaching. The wide-spread improvement in home life throughout the country would depend on well-trained cookery teachers, particularly since the Education Code of 1875 now permitted school boards to include cookery lessons within their curriculum.

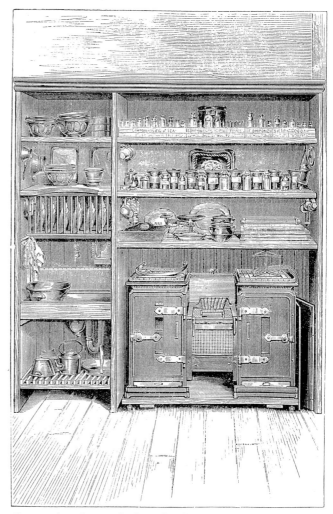

Since cookery lessons had to take place in existing classrooms, Mrs Buckton introduced these splendid cookery cupboards into eight schools in the 1870s. Here we see one of them with its doors and three trestle tables removed ready for use. To the left is a sink, drying rack and storage shelves, while the shelves to the right, above the baking utensils and ingredients, are trays which contain the substances to demonstrate the composition of one pound of tea, of potatoes, and of cocoa.

As early as 1873 Mrs Kitson and Mrs Buckton had carried the Yorkshire Ladies' pioneering engineering educational work into the Leeds Board Schools, Mrs Buckton teaching the girls elementary science, physiology, and food studies at volunteer classes held after school hours. In 1876 the Leeds School Board asked the Leeds School to organise lessons in cleaning and cookery for about 60 of its pupils during normal school hours. Although there were some administrative problems, the practical value of these lessons became immediately apparent, since they enabled the girls to take care of their homes, give their fathers, brothers and sisters comfortable meals, and nurse their mothers or any other members of the family when sick. Hopefully the children would all pass the information and recipes they learned in this way on to their mothers, thus improving the health and well-being of the whole community.

By the late 1870s the Board had adopted these classes, Mrs Buckton, elected on to the Board as its only lady member in 1873, effectively establishing all the required facilities. Her teachers' handbook *Food and Home Cookery, a Course of Instruction in Practical Cookery and Cleaning, for Children Elementary Schools of the Leeds School Board* of 1879 was very successful, new additions appearing in 1883 and 1890.[3] In it she set down full details of this extremely advanced, efficient and workable scheme. Classrooms in eight schools were fitted with cookery cupboards which were excellent examples of Victorian design and practicality. They contained everything from the worktables, utensils, foodstuffs and chemistry apparatus required for the lessons, to a sink and even a gas-powered cooking range specially designed and manufactured for this purpose by Charles Wilson of the Carlton Works, Woodhouse Lane. Every cookery course started with the selection and cleaning of household equipment, then going on to study baking, roasting, frying, soups, invalid cookery, diet and clothing, each section having a theoretical introduction,

This amazing device, "the most compact Gas Kitchener ever seen", was manufactured especially for school use by Charles Wilson at the Carlton Works, Woodhouse Lane. It had two ovens, two sets of boiling rings, and burners which imitated a coal grate to boil, grill and roast by radiant heat. Mounted on wheels, and with a flexible gas-pipe, it could be moved around the room by the teacher, and could be used where there were no facilities for lighting a coal fire.

admirably suited to the girls' level of knowledge, and then illustrated by demonstrations and experiments. These were followed by practical cookery sessions, the resulting dishes being sold at cost price to the girls, who then took them home to their parents. All the recipes were specially printed on separate sheets which were handed round during each lesson, so that the girls could concentrate their attention on the practical activities. They were also encouraged to stick these recipes into personal notebooks, thus building up useful and

legible cookery books, both for their mothers to read at home, and for their own use during the rest of their lives. Although the late 19th century's view of what constituted a good diet is rather different from ours today, no one could accuse Mrs Buckton of providing recipes which were not both substantial, satisfying and extremely economical, as may be seen in the following suggested menu:

Breakfast: porridge with treacle, 300ml/½pt of new milk, or coffee with milk for girls, bread and butter without limit.
Dinner: soup, if no pudding is to be served, e.g.:

Carrot Soup

1.2l/2pt water	*2 potatoes*
50g/2oz carrots	*50g/2oz flour*
1 onion	*50g/2oz dripping*
1 lettuce	*300ml/½pt milk*
2.5ml/½tsp sugar	*salt & pepper to taste*

Finely chop all the vegetables, mix the flour into the dripping, add the remaining ingredients, except the milk, to a saucepan, simmer gently for an hour, stir in the milk, and serve.

main course of:
1. A joint of roast meat.
2. Potatoes boiled in their skins because "the skin of a potato prevents any water from entering the potato, and also prevents any of the juices and good things from getting out". If the potatoes were to be mashed, they were then to be dried, peeled, and beaten with a little dripping or butter, salt and milk.
3. Fresh vegetables such as cabbage, cauliflowers or peas, etc.

puddings, such as:

Baked Rice Pudding

50g/2oz pudding rice	*25g/1oz brown sugar*
600ml/1pt milk	

Mix the ingredients together in an ovenproof dish, and bake at 160°C, 300°F, gas mark 2 for two hours, stirring after the first 30 minutes.

Baked Fruit Pudding

225g/8oz plain flour	*90ml/6tbs (approx) water*
75g/3oz suet	*450g/1lb apples or rhubarb*
a pinch of salt	*50g/2oz sugar*

1. *Peel, core and slice the apples, wash and chop the rhubarb into short lengths.*
2. *Mix the flour, suet and salt with just sufficient water to form a soft dough and roll out 15mm/½in thick.*
3. *Use two-thirds of the pastry to line a greased 850ml/1½pt pudding basin, place the apple or rhubarb inside, sprinkling it with the sugar, wet the edges of the pastry, and apply the remaining pastry to form a lid.*
4. *Bake at 150°C, 300°F, gas mark 2 for 2 hours. Alternatively the top of the pudding may be covered with a piece of pleated greaseproof paper, tied down, and steamed for 2 hours, in which case the sugar should be omitted.*

Tea: half a pint of warm or cold new milk, tea for girls, if required, but with plenty of milk, bread and butter in unlimited quantity.
Supper: bread and cheese.

All these meals were designed to provide the appropriate quantities of starches and fats required as "body warmers", organic matter, gluten, albumen and gum as "flesh formers, and the lime, phosphorus and gelatin necessary to "make our bones grow strong and hard". Other recipes to support these processes included:

Tripe & Onions

450g/1lb dressed tripe	*450g/1lb onions*
milk and water	*15ml/1tbs plain flour*
	575ml/1pt tmilk
	salt and pepper to taste

1. *Boil the tripe for 5 minutes in sufficient milk and water to cover it, then simmer for 2 hours, or until tender.*
2. *Peel and slice the onions, simmer them in a little water for 20 minutes, until tender.*
3. *Beat the flour into a little of the milk, add the rest of the milk in a separate saucepan and bring to the boil while stirring. Add the salt and pepper and the onions, simmer them together for 5 minutes.*
4. *Drain the tripe, and serve it with the onion sauce.*

The educational work carried out by the Yorkshire Training School of Cookery proved extremely successful, and within a few years the Leeds School Board decided to build on these sound foundations by appointing its own teaching staff. In 1897 Miss McCulloch, the Board's Superintendent of Cookery Instruction, published a book of *Cookery Recipes Adopted by the Leeds School Board*.[4] This proved so useful that it was later re-published by E. J. Arnold of Leeds as *The "A.L." Cookery Recipes* to accompany the series of wall-charts, exercise books, teachers' log-books and record books and other cookery books which they published for distribution to education authorities throughout Britain. The recipes were "considered to be one of the best collections to be found in a small book of this kind [and] are now in use all over the country". At first sight her recipes appear very similar to Mrs Buckton's, but in reality they are much lighter, particularly through the use of raising agents, more interesting and more palatable. They include salads, salad dressings, sauces, cakes, biscuits, and even a helpful selection of recipes for the girls of the newly-arrived Jewish community:

Meat Cimez (Jewish)

450g/1lb beef or mutton	*15ml/1tbs black treacle*
450g/1lb potatoes	*300ml/½pt water*
450g/1lb carrots	*salt to taste*
1 turnip	

1. *Cut the meat into 2.5cm/1in cubes, and dice the vegetables.*
2. *Fill a lidded casserole with alternate layers of mixed vegetables and meat, then add the water, treacle and salt.*
3. *Bake at 180°C, 350°F, gas mark 4 for 1 hour 30 minutes to 2 hours.*

Blinces (Jewish)

450g/1lb potatoes	*oil for frying*
1 small egg, beaten	*salt & pepper to taste*
100g/4oz plain flour	

1. *Wash, peel, and finely grate the potatoes into a bowl, add the egg and seasoning, then sift in the flour while stirring the mixture, to produce a soft dough.*

2. *Roll tablespoonfuls of the mixture in flour, flatten them into small round cakes, and fry on both sides in a little oil to a golden brown. It is best to carefully wipe out the pan with a little crumpled kitchen paper between batches, to remove any browned flour which would give a burned taste.*

Stewed Steak

450g/1lb steak	*2 medium onions*
25g/1oz dripping	*2 carrots*
25g/1oz flour	*1 turnip*
600ml/1pt water or stock	

1. *Cut the steak into 2.5cm/1in cubes, peel and slice the onions, carrots and turnip.*
2. *Heat the dripping in a frying pan, lightly fry the steak to seal it, then lightly fry the onions, and put them into a lidded casserole with the other vegetables.*
3. *Pour most of the fat out of the pan, put in the flour, stir it while it browns over a gentle heat, then gradually add the water or stock, then pour this over the meat etc.*
4. *Cook at 180°C, 350°F, gas mark 4 for 2 hours.*

Liver & Bacon

450g/1lb lamb's liver, sliced	*1 onion, peeled & sliced*
100g/4oz bacon, sliced	*salt and pepper to taste*
25g/1oz plain flour	*300ml/½pt water*
a little lard for frying	

1. *Fry the bacon and arrange it around a hot dish.*
2. *Roll the liver in the flour, salt and pepper, and fry gently for about 10 min in the bacon fat, and arrange it in the middle of the bacon.*
3. *Fry the onion, add to the liver and bacon, then brown the flour in the pan, add the water, stir until it boils, and finally pour it over the liver and bacon just before serving.*

Caper Sauce (to accompany mutton)

25g/1oz flour	*5ml/1tsp caper liquor*
15ml/1tbs capers	*salt to taste*
300ml/½pt light stock or water	

Mix the flour with a little cold water in a saucepan, add the remaining stock or water gradually, stirring well, heat, while stirring, until it boils, add salt to taste, and stir in the halved capers and the liquor in which they were pickled.

Parsley Sauce (for fish)

12g/½oz butter	*10ml/2tsp chopped parsley*
15ml/1tbs plain flour	*salt and pepper to taste*
300ml/½pt fish stock, milk or water	

Melt the butter in the pan, stir in the flour, and when quite smooth add the fish stock, etc., and cook, stirring continuously until it boils, then add the parsley and salt and pepper

Macaroni Pudding

50g/2oz macaroni	*1 egg*
600ml/1pt milk	*a little nutmeg, grated*
15ml/1tbs sugar	*pinch of salt*

1. *Boil the macaroni in water for about 20 min, until quite tender, then drain, add the milk and salt, and simmer for a further 10 minutes.*
2. *Beat the egg with the sugar in a small basin, scald with some of the milk from the macaroni, stir it into the macaroni, pour it into a greased pie-dish, grate nutmeg over the top, and bake at 170°C, 325°F, gas mark 3 for 15-20 minutes.*

Ginger Pudding

325g/12oz plain flour	1 egg
75g/3oz suet	300ml/½pt milk
225g/8oz golden syrup	5ml/1tsp baking powder
50g/2oz sugar	5ml/1tsp ground ginger

1. Mix all the dry ingredients in a bowl, break in the egg, add the syrup, and work in with the milk, added little by little, to form a smooth mixture.
2. Grease a large pudding bowl, pour in the mixture, cover with greased and pleated greaseproof paper, tie down, and steam for 2 hours 30 minutes.
3. The pudding may be served with a sweet white sauce and a little grated orange or lemon peel.

Plain Salad

1 lettuce	radishes
a little cress	a small onion

Wash the vegetables in cold water, break up the lettuce and cress with the fingers, cut the radishes and onions into small pieces, and toss with the following:

Salad Sauce

1 hard-boiled egg yolk	5ml/1tsp white sugar
30ml/2tbs olive oil	2.5ml/½tsp made mustard
30ml/2tbs vinegar	pepper and salt to taste

Using the back of a spoon, bring all the dry ingredients together against the inside of a small bowl, then work in the oil very gradually, followed by the vinegar, to produce a smooth, creamy dressing.

Feather Cake

This cake featured in the local version of the song *Billy-boy*, in which the potential bridegroom is questioned about his wife to be:

> Can she cook and can she bake, Billy-boy, Billy-boy?
> Can she cook and can she bake, Charlie-Willie?
> She can cook and she can bake,
> Aye, and make a Feather Cake,
> But she's young, and she can't leave her Mammy.

225g/8oz plain flour	2.5ml/½tsp baking powder
100g/4oz sugar	2.5ml/½tsp bicarbonate of soda
1 egg, beaten	25g/1oz butter
5ml/1tsp cream of tartar	150ml/¼pt milk

1. Pre-heat the oven to 180°C, 350°F, gas mark 4.
2. Rub the butter into the flour, add the sugar, baking powder, cream of tartar, bicarbonate of soda, and egg, mixing in sufficient milk to form a smooth, light mixture.
3. Pour into a greased and floured 20cm/8in round tin, and bake for 30-40 minutes.

Wheatmeal Scones

450g/1lb wheatmeal	small pinch of salt
75g/1oz lard or butter	2.5ml/½tsp bicarbonate of soda

5ml/1tsp cream of tartar	275ml/½pt milk

1. Pre-heat the oven to 200°C, 400°F, gas mark 6.
2. Rub the flat into the flour, add the cream of tartar, bicarbonate of soda and salt, and mix it to a firm paste with the milk.
3. Roll out on a floured board to about 15mm/½in thickness, cut into 75cm/3in rounds, and bake for about 15 minutes. Their appearance may be improved by brushing their tops with milk before baking.

Oatmeal Biscuits

150g/6oz fine or medium oatmeal	
150g/6oz plain flour	7.5ml/½tbs baking powder
100g/4oz sugar	45ml/3tbs [approx] milk
50g/2oz dripping or lard	a pinch of salt

1. Pre-heat the oven to 180°C, 350°F, gas mark 4.
2. Rub the fat into the dry ingredients, make a well in the centre, and work in just sufficient milk to form a stiff paste, roll this out some 3cm/⅛in thick, cut out in 75cm/3in rounds, and bake on lightly greased baking trays for about 15 minutes until a pale golden brown.

From the 1880s and '90s, teachers trained at the Yorkshire Training School were being employed both by the school itself, or by various school boards, to teach classes of school children. They also began to take up more responsible positions, Miss Amy Atkinson working for the Leeds Council of Education and Batley Technical School, for example, and Miss Grace Holroyd becoming Principal of the Bradford School of Cookery and Laundry Work. Both held first-class diplomas from the Leeds School, and in 1900 they combined their professional expertise to write *Practical Cookery, A Collection of Reliable Recipes*, of which 12 editions were published by Nutt & Co of Leeds up to the 1920s.[5] In addition to the usual range of basic recipes, they now included those for "superior" middle-class dishes, such as lobster creams, fillets of beef à la Française, pheasant à la Marlborough, souffles, meringues, hand-made sweets, etc. In all, there were some 675 recipes to meet the needs of all Leeds families, in addition to advice on how to cook with the increasingly popular gas stoves, and similar useful household hints.

By this time the foresight and organising energy of the Yorkshire Ladies had achieved most of their original objectives, since the local education authority now provided lessons in domestic science in virtually every school, and since 1907 had assumed responsibility for teacher training in this subject. From 1921 their school became the Yorkshire Training College of Housecraft, which eventually merged with Leeds Polytechnic in 1966. This was a very impressive achievement, and provides an excellent example of how a group of ladies in Victorian Leeds could not only identify real social needs, but plan an effective solution, and develop it into a state of flourishing success, years before they were even given the right to vote in either local or national elections.

Notes:
1. quoted in Revd N. Price, "Cooking in Public Elementary Schools", *Journal of the Society of Arts*, no.1294 (Sept.1877) 932
2. I. Jenkins, "The Yorkshire Ladies' Council of Education", *Thoresby Society*, LVI Leeds (1981) 27-71
3. E. Driver, *A Bibliography of Cookery Books Published in Britain 1875-1914*, (1989) 145-6
4. *ibid.*, 402
5. *ibid.*, 82

CHAPEL TEAS

AS IN most great cities, the churches and chapels of Victorian and Edwardian Leeds played a major part in the social life of the whole community. In the church halls and school-rooms of the Bethels, Rehobeths, Salems and Zions, a social or religious event was often taking place on virtually every day of the week throughout the entire year. They ranged from prayer meetings, Sunday Schools, Bright Hours and Christian Endeavours, to talks, Band of Hope meetings, the choir, the Boy's Brigade, and the Scouts. Further meetings were required to make all the necessary arrangements for the regular cycle of annual celebrations, the Christmas pantomimes and children's treats, the Whitsuntide walks, the chapel anniversaries, and the grand bazaars.

Careful preparations were essential for all of these, as the ladies of the congregations took great pride in the quality of their catering, especially since their scores or even hundreds of guests and customers would be comparing their efforts with those provided by neighbouring chapels. Most of the baking was home-made, particular ladies often being asked to provide the delicate sponge cakes, rich chocolate cakes, etc., for which they had acquired a fine local reputation. Having assembled the bakery, the ladies then began the mammoth task of slicing and buttering vast quantities of bread and butter, then spreading it with potted meats and fish pastes to produce plate after plate of sandwiches as the atmosphere of the kitchen became increasingly hot and humid with the steam of boiling tea urns.

Whit Monday was the great day for the Sunday Schools, when the scholars of both Anglican and Nonconformist congregations walked in procession around their own locality, singing outside the homes of leading members of their community. In south Leeds Richard Spencer recorded that:[1]

> Early on this joyous morn,
> What beauteous articles are borne
> Through the streets with utmost care,
> Teapots, urns and china-ware,
> Jugs of sweet delicious cream,
> Glitter in the sun's bright beam
> Great tin boilers, you may see,
> To boil the water for the tea.

By early afternoon all the children were assembled, each looking as smart and clean as economically possible in the new clothes which were to last them at least for the coming year. Writing in the 1870s, John Batty described how "It is certainly a charming sight to see the children muster in so large a number, and so well-dressed and clean, it is also a delight to hear their sweet singing of the appointed hymns – the latter especially encouraged by the Methodists – and performed at intervals along the route. After being regaled with tea and buns, they proceed to some field, where toys, oranges and balls are distributed and innocent games played". Once the specially-printed hymn-sheets had been distributed, perhaps a harmonium lifted on to a horse-drawn cart to provide accompaniment, and the smaller children probably seated on flat carts etc., loaned by local farmers and traders, the procession set off:

> Now are the schools of various sections
> Passing on in all directions:
> Some in groups are loudly singing,
> Other sweetest stains are hymning:
> Then on they pass through streets and lanes
> Adorned with orange-stalls and canes,
> And heaps of variegated spice,
> All looking very sweet and nice,
> At which the little ones are peeping
> With fingers in their pockets creeping:
> For some, it seems, won't be content
> Until that little coin is spent:
> But how to spend that Whit-tide penny
> They scarce know 'mongst so many:
> And wearily they lag behind
> But cheered along by teachers kind,
> Who speak of tea so much desired
> They make them quite forget they're tired.

Meanwhile, back at the schoolroom, the ladies were busily employed in preparing the tea for the patrons and teachers of the schools, and for the children, the tables being set up out of doors if there was a field close at hand, and the weather was fine. Here the sandwiches, cakes and buns might be arranged on large plates for the returning children, but, from experience, many chapels found it less troublesome to distribute the food in individual paper bags, so that each child was sure to receive its fair share. If there was insufficient crockery, everybody brought their own mugs etc., these being clearly identified by strands of coloured threads wound around their handles. Thus prepared, grace was sung:

> Be present at our table Lord, Be here and everywhere adored,
> Thy creatures bless, and grant that we May dine in Paradise with thee. Amen.

Then the tea was served from the trestle tables, and the rest of the long day spent in sport and games.

At other times throughout the year the chapels celebrated their anniversaries by inviting neighbouring congregations to join them for an afternoon during which a popular minister or lay preacher conducted a service of hymns, readings, etc., usually followed by a splendid tea provided, as always, by the ladies.

The same ladies also used their considerable experience of catering to raise funds for their church or chapel, a single October Tea organised by the Lady Lane Sabbath School in 1886 producing over £20 clear profit from collections, subscriptions, the sale of provisions and tickets.[2] Most income was generated by the annual bazaars, at which a great variety of goods either made by the congregations, donated by local people, or obtained from commercial suppliers were offered for sale on gaily decorated stalls set up around the schoolroom. During the Edwardian period these were extremely grand, colourful and popular affairs, frequently continuing for perhaps four days at a time. Every year a different overall theme would be chosen, which dictated the choice of decoration and associated events. Just before World War One, for example, Belle Vue Methodists in Burley patriotically chose "Britain and her Colonies", with the refreshment stall and cafe representing Canada.[3] Here "The young ladies of the Sunday School and Institute will serve as Cafe Maidens" offering "Meat Tea 9d, Plain Tea 6d, Supper 9 to 10 pm 6d each." The bazaar might also feature bakery competitions, such as that organised at the Lady Lane Central Mission by the "Ladies of the School and Congregation", which had classes for "Bread and Teacakes" on Wednesday, "Scones and Biscuits" on Thursday, and "Apple Pies on Plates and Gingerbread" on Saturday.[4] Further income was generated by the sale of specially-printed recipe books compiled by the ladies, these frequently including such specialities as:[5]

Scripture Cake

4½ cups	I Kings chapter iv, verse 22	plain flour	125g/5oz
1½ cups	Judges v,25	butter	50g/2oz
2 cups	Jeremiah vi, 20 last clause	sugar	100g/4oz
2 cups	I Samuel xxi, 12	raisins	75g/3oz
2 cups	Nahum iii,12	currants	75g/3oz
2tbs	I Samuel xiv, 25	honey	10ml/2tsp
1 cup	Numbers xvii, 8	flaked almonds	50g/2oz
to taste	II Chronicles ix, 9	mixed spice	2.5ml/½tsp
6	Jeremiah xvii, ii	eggs	2
a pinch	Leviticus iv, 19	salt	pinch
3tsp	Amos iv, 5	baking powder	5ml/1tsp

Follow Soloman's advice for making a good boy, Proverbs xxiii, 14 ["thou beatest him with a rod"] and you will have a good cake.
1. For an 18cm/7in round tin,use the quantities in the right-hand column.
2. Pre-heat the oven to 170°C, 325°F, gas mark 3, and line the tin with greased greaseproof paper.
3. Cream the butter with the sugar, beat in the honey, then the eggs and the milk.
4. Sift together the flour, baking powder, mixed spice and salt, and fold these into the mixture.
5. Gently stir in the fruit and almonds, pour into the tin, and bake for 1 hour 15 minutes.

Married Woman Cake[6]

1lb of true love	1lb of perfect trust and confidence
1lb of cheerfulness	a pinch of unselfishness

a sprinkle of interest in all your husband does
Mix all these with 1 gill of oil of sympathy: put in a tin of contentment, flavour with a bright fireside and a loving kiss: bake well all your life.

Some of the income raised in this way was used to provide the ladies with funds to help the elderly and the infirm, Belgrave Congregational Church holding monthly "At Homes" with teas and entertainments for the over-65s, as well as an excellent Annual Treat for over 500 people every January.[7] The quality of the chapel teas may be judged by trying the following recipes published for the Young Ladies' Stall at the "Gratitude" Bazaar, Waterloo Road Wesleyan Church, Hunslet, in 1915:

Potted Beef, Mrs Willie Ingamells
Take 450g/1lb of shin beef and cover it nicely with water and stew two or three hours slowly, then chop it finely and season to taste with salt, pepper and mace.

Polony, Mrs W. E. Huckerby
Originating from the Bologna sausages of the 17th century, polony sausages are still made by Leeds pork butchers, their smooth textured meat and cereal filling being enclosed in a bright red skin. They were cooked by the butcher, and only needed slicing at home.

450g/1lb lean beef	100g/4oz fesh white breadcrumbs
225g/8oz lean ham	1 egg
5ml/1tsp dried sage	salt and pepper to taste

1. Mince the beef and ham together very finely, and mix thoroughly with the remainder of the ingredients to form a stiff paste, and knead this into a round ball.
2. Tie the polony tightly into a piece of flannel or cotton and boil for 2 hours 30 minutes. Remove the cloth, allow to cool, and slice thinly for sandwiches etc.

Courting Cake, Miss B. Morrison

275g/10oz plain flour	75g/3oz butter
225g/8oz sugar	1 egg, beaten
7.5ml/½tbs baking powder	75ml/⅛pt milk [approx]
2.5ml/½tsp bicarbonate of soda	raspberry jam

1. Pre-heat the oven to 180°C, 350°F, gas mark 4.
2. Mix together all the dry ingredients, rub in the butter, and mix in the egg with just sufficient milk to form a pastry, and knead until smooth on a floured board.
3. Divide the pastry into two, roll out one half and lay it across the base of a 25cm/9in square baking tin, spread this with a layer of raspberry jam to within 2cm/½in of the edges, then roll out the other half of the pastry and place it on top of the jam, damping and sealing the edges.
4. Bake for 20-25 minutes, allow to cool, and then cut into squares.

Sponge Cake, Mrs B. Morrison

4 free range eggs	125g/5oz plain flour
225g/8oz caster sugar	grated rind of 1 lemon

1. Pre-heat the oven to 180°C, 350°F, gas mark 4, and grease and dust with flour the interior of an 18cm/7in round cake tin.
2. Whisk the eggs a little, add the sugar, and whisk thoroughly until very stiff, and light in colour, then fold in the sifted flour and lemon rind as lightly as possible.
3. Pour the mixture into the tin and bake for 45-60 minutes.

Seed Cake, Mrs Raddings, Hunslet

225g/8oz plain flour	2 free range eggs, separated
175g/6oz sugar	5ml/1tsp baking powder
100g/4oz butter	10ml/2tsp carraway seeds
150ml/¼pt milk	

1. Pre-heat the oven to 180°C, 350°F, gas mark 4, and grease and sprinkle with flour the inside of a 18cm/7in round cake tin.
2. Cream the butter with the sugar, beat in the egg yolks, then sift in the milk, little by little, and stir in the seeds. Beat the whites to stiffness, and stir them in lightly
3. pour the mixture into the tin and bake for about 50 minutes.

Date Pastry, Mrs H. Dixon, Grove Road

225g/8oz plain flour	7.5ml/½tbs baking powder
100g/4oz lard	pinch of salt

225g/8oz dates   2.5ml/½tsp sugar

1. Pre-heat the oven to 220°C, 425°F, gas mark 7.
2. Stone the dates and gently stew with 150ml/¼pt water for about 5 minutes, stirring occasionally, until soft.
3. Rub the lard into the dry ingredients and mix in 15ml/1tbs water (approx) to form the pastry, divide this in two, and roll out each piece to around 23cm/9ins square.
4. Place one piece of pastry on a baking sheet, spread with the dates, leaving a narrow margin around the sides, damp this margin, place the other piece of pastry on top as a lid, turn the edges over to seal them, prick the lid with a fork, and bake for 15 minutes.
5. Cut into squares when cold.

Apple Snow, Mrs T. Taylor, Ivy Dene, Cross Flatts Avenue

4 trifle sponges	450g/1lb peeled & cored apple
30ml/2tbs sugar	3 sterilised egg whites
3 egg yolks, beaten	pinch of salt
425ml/¾pt milk	175g/6oz sugar
grated peel and juice of 1 lemon	

1. Bring the milk to the boil, and pour it over the eggs, lemon peel and sugar in a saucepan, stir over a gentle heat until it has thickened, but do not approach boiling or it will curdle.
2. Cut the sponge into small cubes, arrange them across the bottom of a large dish, cover it with the slightly cooled custard, and leave it to go cold.
3. Stew the apples until tender in their own juice (or with very little water), then mash with a fork to form a smooth puree.
4. Whisk the egg whites with the salt until very stiff, then beat in the sugar, apple puree and lemon juice until stiff, and finally heap this mixture over the custard and serve cold.

Cheesecakes, or curd tarts were another favourite for Chapel teas. The curds, made from skim-milk and resembling cottage cheese, but with a drier taste and consistency, were sold by most grocers and in the markets, and are stocked by some supermarkets today. At home the curd tarts were baked as follows:

Curd Cheesecakes

225g/8oz curds	50g/2oz currants
2 eggs, beaten	30ml/2tbs double cream
100g/4oz melted butter	2.5ml/½tsp grated nutmeg
100g/4oz sugar	grated peel of 1 lemon [optional]
225g/8oz shortcrust pastry	

1. Pre-heat the oven to 180°C, 350°F, gas mark 4.
2. Roll out the pastry, and use it to line a number of deep tart tins, or shallw flan tins.
3. Mix all the remaining ingredients together, fill the pastry cases two-thirds full, and bake for 30-35 minutes.

Cheesecakes similar to these were also a speciality of Cheesecake House, a late-medieval timber-framed house just south of Oulton. In the 1890s it was occupied by a joiner, Matthew Brook, whose wife and daughters Mary and Jane made the cheesecakes, a billy and two nanny goats browsing in its rural garden ensuring a continuous supply of rich milk to make the creamiest of curds. The cheesecakes, along with puff pastries and vanilla slices, were baked both in a Yorkshire range and a stone "beehive" oven at its side, and then sold with other refreshments to wagonette and charabanc parties which used to drive here from the neighbouring towns and villages, a continuation of the Georgian tea-garden tradition.

Notes:
1. R. Spencer, *Field Flowers*, Batley, (1890) 86
2. Leeds Local History Library LP 287
3. Belle Vue Methodist Church, *Grand Bazaar, Britain and her Colonies*, Leeds (1914)
4. Lady Lane Central Mission, *Annual Bazaar, 5-8 December 1917*, Leeds (1917)
5. A. Atkins & G. Holroyd, *Practical Cookery*, Leeds (6th ed. 1911) 151
6. *Gratitude Bazaar, 1915, Recipe Book issued in connection with the Young Ladies' Stall*, Leeds (1915)
7. *Belgrave Congregational Church Annual Report, 1923*, Leeds (1923)

VICTORIAN PROSPERITY

AS LEEDS became a great industrial city, it developed a large and prosperous middle class which drew its income either through operating huge textile, engineering, leather or chemical works, or who provided legal, financial, medical or other professional services to the whole community. In the early 19th century most of them still lived in the elegant Georgian west end, around Park Square etc., and the villas scattered in the still rural countryside within a mile of the town centre. By the 1850s the expansion of the town centre, the construction of heavy industry up the Aire Valley, the increasing use of coal to power steam engines and heat thousands of small homes, and the fouling of the river, meant that this once idyllic location was now polluted beyond endurance. As a result, all those who could afford to do so looked for pastures new, the obvious location for middle-class housing developments now being the small village of Headingley, centred on its old chapel, Shire Oak and public houses, set on a broad ridge offering delightful views over the Aire and Meanwood valleys. Here, and in other still undeveloped areas from Armley in the west to Roundhay in the east, hundreds of fine villas and terraces were built from the 1830s to the 1900s. Although some have since been demolished or split into flats, and had their grounds re-developed with largely post-war semis, they are still to be found here in large numbers, providing Leeds with some of its best residential properties.

In a number of houses, particularly the terraces, kitchens remained at cellar level for some time, their sinks and iron ranges still occasionally being found in situ. In most villas, however, the kitchen was at ground level, forming part of the servants' wing, but located close to the dining room for ease of service. The better houses had a greatly improved arrangement, however, with the kitchen built as a separate single-storey room connected to the cool northern elevation, its

walls being largely solid to give maximum workspace, while ample light and ventilation were provided by a pyramidal glazed roof. Good examples can be seen at Crooked Acres on Abbey Walk, or Ford House off Headingley Lane.

The suites of kitchen offices included keeping cellars, larders and pantries, back kitchens or sculleries for all the dirty work and washing up, and the kitchen itself. Large Yorkshire or similar ranges provided all the facilities for the actual cooking, the charcoal stoves now being replaced by the much more convenient gas rings, companies such as John Beverley of Mark Lane, established in 1827, making iron gas stoves with boiling rings on top from the mid 1860s.[1]

As for the equipment, we can obtain very detailed descriptions from the catalogues of various house-contents sales carried out by local auctioneers from the 1850s.[2] In the centre of the room stood a large oak-, sycamore or deal-topped table fitted with drawers, where all the work was carried out using, among numerous other items, graters, spoons, pastry and chopping boards, sieves, and the locally-made brown, black or cream-glazed mixing bowls, known here as pancheons. Steel hatchets and nippers were used to break up the sugar loaves

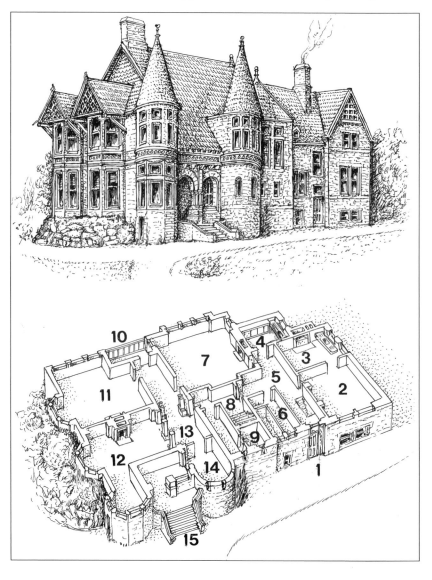

In 1871, George Corson, the fashionable Leeds architect, built "Dunearn" on Wood Lane, Headingley, for his own use. He was skilled in villa design, building a number of similar scale around north Leeds. The ground floor of his house included:

1. Servant's entrance
2. Kitchen (over wash-house)
3. Scullery
4. Butler's Pantry
5. Dinner-service lobby & servant's stair
6. Store Room
7. Dining Room
8. Principal Stairs
9. Lavatory
10. Verandah
11. Drawing Room
12. Morning Room
13. Hall
14. Porch
15. Main Entrance

The larger villas built their kitchens in northern wings with pyramid-shaped roofs to provide the required levels of light and ventilation. These examples are seen at Crooked Acres at Kirkstall (left), and Ford House off Headingley Lane (right).

into smaller lumps, and pestles and mortars to reduce them to powder, while saws and chopping knives were used to prepare meat for cooking. Around the table, and by the fire, stood three or four Windsor, elm or beech chairs, along with a rocking chair for the front kitchen also served as a servants' hall for the domestic staff.

For roasting, brass bottle jacks rotated the joints in front of the open firebars, the juices falling into a dripping tin from which they could be basted back over the meat. Sometimes the meat was backed by a tin-lined wooden roasting screen, which both reflected the fire's heat back on to the meat, and serves as a very practical hot-cupboard, but in other households a tin "hastener" was used, this being a half-round tin screen which incorporated both the bottle-jack and the dripping pan in a single convenient unit. This equipment, backed up with the copper saucepans, brass pans, large fish and turbot kettles, preserving pans and tea kettles, etc., all guaranteed that food could be cooked as efficiently as possible, the kitchen clock ensuring that meals could always appear on the table with great punctuality.

Before proceeding to the dining room, we must first look at a unique dispute between a cook and her employer which took place in a house in Park Square in February 1865, and resulted in the famous Leeds Dripping Riot. For generations most cooks, and most employers, believed that the dripping left after roasting the meat was a perquisite of the cook, who could give it away or sell it as she chose. However, her employer, a local doctor and magistrate, took exception to this practice, took her to a private court, and had her thrown into Armley Gaol for a month for stealing his dripping. The public were outraged, and the prison authorities, fearing trouble on her release, sent her out from prison early in the morning to catch the 7am train to Scarborough. Between 8 and 9am the mob assembled outside the gaol, hurling snowballs, sticks and stones, but on finding

Gas stoves were made in Leeds by firms such as John Beverley of Mark Lane and Charles Wilson of Carlton Works, Woodhouse Lane, from the mid-Victorian period. This advertisement from Turner's hardware stores in Lower Briggate shows one in a modern kitchen of 1904.

that their heroine had departed, they began to assemble outside the house in Park Square, two men parading outside with a physic bottle and a frying pan on a long pole. Now the Mayor made a call for help to Bradford for extra police, and to the Lord Mayor of York for two troops of cavalry, the 16th Lancers arriving by special train just before 5pm. Two hours later, two thousand people had to be cleared from the front of the Town Hall, where George Hudson, a potter, was knocked down and fatally injured in the crush. As for the magistrate, he quite properly became the subject of popular derision, as described in verses such as:[3]

> Nah t'month e Armley gaol is past
> An' sho cums aght agean at last,
> While throo each rooad, an' lane, an' street,
> The public this poor servant meet,
> An' show their luv ov truth an' right
> Aggean this would-be man of right!
> > Drippin, drippin, drippin,
> > Noa perquisite, noa tippin.

or, to the tune of *The Ratcatcher's Daughter*:[4]

> In Leeds there lived not long ago,
> A Justice of the Peace:
> He was a doctor by his trade,
> And wasn't he fond of grease!
> He had a Cook – a jolly Cook,
> Eliza was her name:
> She took bad fat from off his meat,
> And rendered down the same
> Chorus: Drippin oh! dripping ho!
> > Oh don't I love my dripping.
> Says Eliza, "This 'ere fat's my own
> A cookey's per-qui-site"
> For she had never understood
> That might must bow to might
> So when this Justice of the Peace
> Who was Eliza's master,
> Heard that she had took his grease,
> There came a sad disaster.
> Chorus:
> Says he to Cook "I've got you now,
> And don't begin your fibbing:
> You've took my fat from off my meat,
> And boiled it down for dripping.
> As a Magistrate I know the law,
> I'll call in the Police,
> And send you into durance vile,
> For taking of my grease."
> Chorus:
> Poor Cookey she was dragged away
> Into a private court,
> But before she could say "Jack Robinson"
> She was completely floor'd …
> So for a month in Armley Gaol
> You will be kept quite tight,
> And dripping never take again,
> As your own per-qui-site.
> Chorus:
> Now all you cooks and servant gals
> Wot's very fond of "tipping",
> Don't take your master's scraps of fat
> And boil 'em down for dripping:

> For if you do, bear this in mind,
> The Magistrates won't fail
> To try you in a private court,
> And send you off to gaol.
> Chorus:

The dining rooms in the prosperous Leeds houses in the 1850s represented settings of substantial comfort and quality. The room itself was covered in Brussels carpet, with rich red, crimson or maroon curtains of wool, alpacca or silk damask, sometimes hung from gilded cornices. On one wall, an elaborate fireplace displayed polished steel fire irons and fenders, while around the others were a long Spanish mahogany sideboard, with a matching cellarette for chilling the wines, a sofa, easy chairs and perhaps a bookcase, and either a circular dumb waiter, or a dinner-waggon. The dining table, of Spanish mahogany like all the other furniture, worked on the telescopic principle, extra leaves enabling it to extend up to 14ft by 4ft 8in wide. Normally its colour and polish were preserved beneath a cover made of green cloth, or scarlet and black plaid, but in use it was covered with the finest linen damask, beautifully laundered, starched and ironed. For the diners, suites of six to 12 chairs were quite normal, some being of the fashionable "Grecian" design, their upholstered seats being covered in black horsehair, maroon morocco leather, or even crimson Utrecht velvet. The glowing richness of the predominantly red colour scheme, with the polished mahogany, all lit by the soft, warm light from the bronze oil-lamps provided an excellent foil for the pure white tablecloth, with its glittering array of cut glass, fine silverware, and beautiful services of transfer-printed earthenware, ironstone china, or porcelain.[5] Leeds could provide some of the finest dining rooms in England. When William Fairbairn entertained Queen Victoria at his home at Woodsley Hall, Clarendon Road, it was reported that his "dining-room is one of the most perfect little bijous in the Italian style to be met with in any provincial town".[6]

Later in the century the mahogany furniture, much of it made by local manufacturers such as Kendall's, later Marsh and Jones, continued to be highly valued, even when 50 or 60 years old. In the more fashionable homes, however, the influence first of the antiquarians, and then the Arts and Crafts movement, brought a renewed interest in furniture made of oak, heavily carved and turned in one of the earlier period styles. At Abbey House, for example, John Octavius Butler used reproduction dark-stained oak in the mid-late Stuart style to furnish his dining room in the twelfth-century gatehouse of Kirkstall Abbey. This was in the 1860s, but by the 1870s sumptuous dining rooms, with moulded plaster ceilings, fine stained glass, and panelled walls, were being incorporated into many of the Headingley villas designed by architects such as George Corson. The finest was probably Spenfield, now the offices of Yorkshire Water. The quality of late Victorian oak dining rooms and their furniture can still be seen today in houses such as Temple Newsam, where Mrs Meynell Ingram employed C. & E. Kempe of London to completely remodel her dining room in 1894.

In the Edwardian period, mahogany furniture in the classic late Georgian styles returned to fashion, beautifully made reproductions, highly finished and French polished, being bought from both local and London furnishers. At Rutland Lodge, for example, Sam Wilson paid Herbert E. Wheeler of Westminster £1,745 to re-design his dining room and to supply a magnificently carved mahogany sideboard for £120.[7] These represent enormous sums in today's values, and clearly reflect the importance that dining, good food, and an active social life played in the business and professional communities of north Leeds.

Unfortunately few of the recipe books or menus used in the wealthier households of Victorian Leeds have yet come to light, but presumably they followed the trends recorded in the fashionable cookery and household management books of the period, such as that of the redoubtable Mrs Beeton. The 1878 recipe book of Ellen Bulmer, probably a housekeeper at St Mark's Villas, near the University, includes many of the fairly plain but substantial dishes associated with her style of cookery.[8] The professional classes were certainly concerned with both their diets and the purity of their foods, however, for subscribers to the Leeds Library acquired books such as *Practical Dietaries for Families* of 1865, *The Manual of Diet in Health and Disease* of 1865, and *Food and Cookery for Infants* of 1884, along with Hassall's 1865 *Food and its Adulteration* and *Foods, their Composition and Analysis* of 1862, which they needed for their guidance.

In the 1830s William Buck set up his business as grocer, coffee roaster and importer of foreign fruits in this shop at 51, Briggate. Later the business continued as Buck and Jackson, and then as William Green and Sons, only ceasing to sell high class groceries for the middle classes when it closed for demolition in 1922.

The Georgian tradition of taking dinner around midday or early afternoon continued in some households well into the 1850s, as described by T. Wemyss Reid in 1883: "Tea at six or half-past six o'clock was the customary meal for which invitations were issued: then came three or four hours for pleasant talk or amusement. Everybody was in the best possible humours for occupations of this kind. Nobody had been made drowsy or

listless by partaking of a heavy meal with a variety of wines, more or less pure: there was no separation of the sexes at the very time when mutual conversation ought to be most enjoyable to both: and it need hardly be said that, in provincial towns at least, there was not the faintest suspicion that a time would come when tobacco would compete with the fair sex for the attention of gentlemen. At the close of the evening thus pleasantly spent, came a meal which gave completeness to the entertainment – supper. It was the custom in Leeds in those days, in the houses of the fashionable, to serve this meal about ten o'clock at a buffet. It was not a heavy meal, and though I am aware of the horror in which the present generation professes to hold for the very idea of supper, I am prepared to maintain that a meal of two courses under this name at ten o'clock is not necessarily more injurious to the digestion than a heavy meal of ten or 12 courses under the name of a dinner, at eight or nine o'clock."[9]

The changes he described were quite revolutionary. The Georgian practice, known as service à la Française, had developed over the years up to the 1850s, still having numerous dishes in each course, but now with some five courses rather than the earlier two. In the first course came soups and fish dishes, followed by an entree course of curries, cutlets, rissoles and savoury stews, etc. In the second course came roast and boiled meats and their accompaniments, followed by a course of game and sweet dishes, a virtual fifth course comprising a dessert of fresh and preserved fruits, ices and similar cold delicacies.

From the 1860s it was increasingly fashionable to use service à la Russe, in which the dishes were not placed on the table as before, but were handed round by a servant to each guest in turn, this method enabling the food to be served piping hot, and to appear in a larger number of contrasting courses. This was the manner in which the late Victorian and Edwardian hostesses served their dinners, for it had the advantage that they could personally supervise the cooking and garnishing of all the cold foods, and see that all the soups and sauces, etc., were made entirely to her satisfaction, and still leave her time to dress for dinner.

Clear evidence that the wives of the Leeds manufacturing and professional classes had a real knowledge and interest in food and cookery is provided by two cookery books written by Mrs Blanche Leigh, her *Souvenir Cookery Book* of 1905 and her *Leeds Household Book* of 1913.[10] The first book was written to raise funds for the Leeds Maternity Home, for both she and her husband, Percival Tookey Leigh, played a very active part in the charitable and public life of the city. She was on the committees of the Leeds Maternity Hospital and the Leeds Babies Welcome, and stood as a candidate for the Leeds Board of Guardians, while he was a City Councillor, Chairman of the Hospital Sub-Committee, and founder of the Leeds Schools Dental Service, later rising to become Lord Mayor in 1935.[11]

At her home "Collina", the fine stone-built villa at 55 Headingley Lane, Mrs Leigh began to collect over 500 recipes from ladies such as Mrs Armitage of Farnley Hall, Mrs Currer-Briggs of Gledhow, Mrs Marshall and Mrs Bray of Headingley, and Mrs Clarke of Hollin House, the wives of the city's leading manufacturers and coal-owners. The recipes show a very high standard of proficiency and good taste, using a wide variety of fresh ingredients to make a range of very flavoursome, attractive and nourishing dishes, as may be seen in the following selection from her recipes chosen to form a complete Edwardian Leeds dinner.

Soup: Summer Soup

2 lettuces	1.8l/2pt vegetable stock
15ml/1tbs butter	1 egg yolk
1 cucumber	150ml/¼pt single cream
300ml/½pt petit pois	salt and pepper to taste

1. Shred the lettuce, put it in a pan with the butter and cook with the lid on until they are soft.
2. Cut the cucumber into small pieces and add it to the lettuce, along with the pea and stock, and simmer for 45 minutes, then add salt and pepper to taste.
3. Beat the egg yolk into the cream, pour this into a tureen, pour the soup on top of it, and serve.

Fish: Crab Salad (for three people)

1 dressed crab	15ml/1tbs whipped cream
1 boiled egg yolk	1 small lettuce, washed
5ml/1tsp olive oil	a little cress or watercress
30ml/2tbs white breadcrumbs	salt, pepper, paprika & vinegar to taste
half a cucumber, sliced	3 tomatoes, sliced

1. Take the dark meat from the shell, mix it with the pounded egg yolk, olive oil, breadcrumbs, and a little salt, pepper and vinegar, mix all together, and form into small balls.
2. Break the claws, remove the white meat, flake it, and mix it with the cream and a little vinegar.
3. Line a dish with small pieces of torn lettuce and a little cress or watercress, edge the dish with small upstanding lettuce leaves.
4. Put the white meat in the centre, and sprinkle it with a little paprica, then surround it with borders of cucumber slices, then tomato slices, and finally, next to the lettuce leaves, the balls of the crab mixture.

Entree: Savoury Pudding

3 large onions	75ml/6tbs suet
60ml/4tbs flour	pinch of salt, of pepper, & of thyme
60ml/4tbs medium oatmeal	2.5ml/½tsp dried sage
60ml/4tbs white breadcrumbs	1 egg

1. Simmer the whole onions for 1 hour 30 min (save the water for soup), chop them finely, and place in a large bowl, then stir in all the remaining ingredients to form a stiff paste.
2. Grease a dripping pan, put in the mixture, forking it level, and bake at 200°C, 400°F, gas mark 6, for 15 minutes and serve immediately with gravy.

Roast: Roast Beef

Accompanied by boiled or mashed potatoes, seasonal vegetables, and:

Parsnip Cakes

625g/1lb 8oz parsnips	15ml/1tbs butter
salt & pepper to taste	1 egg, beaten
30ml/2tbs plain flour	

1. Peel and cut the parsnips in pieces in salted water for 15-20 minutes until soft.
2. Drain and mash the parsnips, mix in the remainder of the ingredients and form them into small cakes.
3. 30 minutes before the beef is ready, bake the cakes either in the dripping tin with the meat, or in a separate greased dish.

Stuffed Onions

900g/2lb Spanish onions	pepper and salt to taste
125g/8oz sausagemeat	15ml/1tbs Yorkshire Relish
15ml/1tbs flour	(use Worcestershire Sauce)

1. Peel the onions and simmer for around 20 min, then drain (retaining the liquor for sauces and soups), place root-end down on a greased baking dish, remove the centres with a fork, but do not break the outsides, and fill the cavity with the sausagemeat, piling any remaining sausage meat on top.
2. Bake at 200°C, 400°F, gas mark 6 for 30-40 minutes.
3. Pour any juices from the baking dish, with 300ml/½pt of the onion liquor, thicken it with 5ml/1tsp cornflour and flavour it with salt and pepper, pour this over the onions, and serve them in the dish in which they were baked.

Horseradish Sauce

30ml/2tbs grated horseradish root	2.5ml/½tsp salt
15ml/1tbs malt vinegar	45ml/3tbs whipped cream

1. Mix together all the ingredients except the cream, and leave them to stand 30 minutes.
2. Stir in the cream just before serving.

Dessert: Orange Salad

6 oranges	30ml/2tbs maraschino
30ml/2tbs sugar	3 bananas
sweet sherry	

1. Peel 3 of the oranges, slice them, and arrange them in layers, with sugar sprinkled between, in a serving dish.
2. Squeeze the juice from the remaining oranges, strain it, add half its volume in sherry, and pour it over the fruit.
3. Slice the peeled bananas across into small rounds and scatter these over and among the oranges, and baste well with the juice.
4. Five minutes before serving, pour the maraschino over the fruit, and serve.

Stewed Dates

225g/8oz whole dried dates	30ml/2tbs dry sherry
100g/4oz sugar	2-3 drops vanilla essence
600ml/1pt water	whipped cream

1. Place the dates, sugar and water in a saucepan, bring to the boil, then keep hot, but below simmering, for 30 minutes.
2. Drain the dates, and put them in a serving dish, rapidly boil the remaining syrup until quite thick, stir in the sherry and vanilla, pour this over the dates, chill them, and serve them with a bowl of whipped cream.

Coffee: Café Turc

450ml/¾pt water	45ml/3tbs ground coffee
30ml/2tbs sugar	

1. Bring the water and sugar to the boil, then put in the coffee, and stir until it boils up.
2. Remove from the heat, tap the pan 3 times with a hard object, re-boil it, and repeat this three times, beating rapidly.
3. Allow the grounds to settle, strain it through a fine sieve, and serve in small, hot cups, with or without cream.

Liqueurs: Orange Brandy

pared zest of 1 orange & 1 lemon	450g/1lb sugar
600ml/1pt brandy	

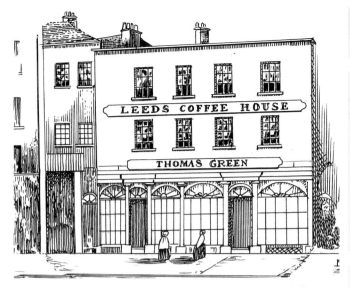

From the 1840s Leeds businessmen could dine on chops, full dinners, coffee and beers at Philip Clarke's Leeds Coffee House at 41 Boar Lane. In 1849 it was taken over by Thomas Green, but was then demolished in 1867 when the whole street was widened and rebuilt as a major shopping centre.

1. *Cut up the zests, and steep them in the brandy in a sealed container for two weeks, shaking it daily.*
2. *Put in the sugar and shake daily for a further fortnight, then store in a cool place for four months, then strain through a coffee filter-paper, and bottle for use.*

Mrs Leigh also collected a selection of recipes of Indian origin which were then being made in local households, these reflecting England's long association with the sub-continent. Some, like kedgeree, had become virtually completely Anglicised by the 1900s, losing their original ingredients, such as dahl. Others, such as the curries and the samosas, were probably as near to the original Indian dishes as it was possible to be when using the ingredients available in England:

Kedgeree (for breakfast)

50g/2oz long-grain rice	*225g/8oz cooked fish*
900ml/1½pt water	*5ml/1tsp anchovy sauce*
5ml/1tsp salt	*50g/2oz butter*
1 egg, beaten	

1. *Bring the water to the boil, add the rice and salt, stir, and cover uncooked 12 minutes, until tender, then drain, rinse, and drain once more.*
2. *Flake the fish, remove the bones, then mix the fish, rice, anchovy and egg together, stir-fry in the butter, and serve immediately.*

Indian Curry

1 onion, chopped	*450g/1lb raw, lean poultry or lamb*
3 cardomoms	*1 tin tomatoes*
10 cloves	*5cm/2ins stick of cinnamon*
30ml/2tbs curry powder	*45ml/2tbs coconut milk*
100g/4oz butter	*10ml/2tsp vinegar*
pinch of salt	

1. *Fry the onions in the butter until pale gold in colour, stir in the spices and curry powder, and cook gently, stirring, for 10 minutes.*
2. *Add the cubed meat, tomatoes, coconut and vinegar, with the minimum of water if necessary, and stew, covered, for 1 hour or until tender, then add salt to taste, and serve with boiled rice.*

Bobotee

600g/1lb cooked beef or mutton	*2.5ml/½tsp curry powder*
1 large onion, finely chopped	*5ml/1tsp chopped blanched almonds*
25g/1oz butter	*2 eggs, beaten*
25g/1oz white breadcrumbs	*salt and pepper to taste*
450ml/¾pt milk	

1. *Fry the onions in the butter, cut the meat into small pieces, and mix in all the remaining ingredients.*
2. *Place in an oven-proof dish, and bake at 200°C, 400°F, gas mark 6, for 15-20 minutes.*

Curried Eggs

50g/2oz long-grain rice	*2.5ml/½tsp curry powder*
6 eggs	*2.5ml/½tsp plain flour*
50g/2oz butter	*60ml/4tbs double cream*
2 onions, sliced	*half a lemon*
300ml/½pt stock	*pinch of salt*

1. *Boil the rice as instructed in the Kedgeree recipe above.*
2. *Fry the onions in the butter until tender, add the stock, curry powder and flour, and simmer gently for 10 minutes, then stir in the salt and cream.*
3. *Boil the eggs for 5 minutes, quarter them, add them into the sauce, pour into a border of rice arranged on a dish, and squeeze the lemon juice over them just before serving.*

Chingaree Puffs, or Samosas

225g/8oz prepared prawns or shrimps, or raw poultry or lean meat in small cubes	*10ml/2tsp curry powder*
	2.5ml/½tsp salt
	275g/10oz plain flour
275g/10oz butter	*50g/2oz sliced onion*

1. *Fry the onions in 50g/2oz of the butter, until pale brown, add the curry powder, prawns and salt, and cook gently until the fish or meat is tender.*
2. *Rub 100g/4oz of the butter into the flour, stir in just sufficient cold water to form a shortcrust pastry, roll it out thinly on a floured board, cut into 8cm/3ins circles, place a portion of the filling on each one, damp the edges, fold over and seal the edges to make small turnovers.*
3. *Melt the remaining butter in a frying pan and fry the puffs until light brown, and serve immediately as an entree.*

Mrs Leigh's interest in cookery extended far beyond the local scene, for she became probably the country's foremost collector of cookery books. Her earliest items were Babylonian tablets of 2500 BC, containing lists of food, ancient Egyptian papyrus showing food offerings to the god Osiris, early printed books from the 1470s, manuscript recipe books, and over 1,500 cookery books, including every major English work, in addition to others in Greek, Latin, Italian, French and German. In 1939 Mrs Leigh, with her characteristic public spirit, gave the entire collection to the Brotherton Library at Leeds University, so that it would become available to everyone who wished to seriously study this fascinating subject. Since then, its presence has attracted very substantial additions, such as the John F. Preston Collection in 1962, so that it is now internationally recognised as the leading food history library in Britain.

In 1973, as a direct result of Mrs Leigh's great gift, Anne Wilson, the Assistant Librarian at the Brotherton, was able to write *Food and Drink in Britain*, the finest comprehensive study of this complex and under-researched subject, while since 1986 the Leeds Symposium on Food History and Traditions has established a national reputation for its pioneering scholarship and publications. This continuing activity is a fitting tribute to Mrs Leigh, and to the experienced lady cooks of her generation.

Before leaving the dining arrangements of the middle classes, it is interesting to look at the facilities they used when visiting the city centre, both for work and for pleasure. Traditionally the inns had provided meals for those who were unable to take their meals at home, these usually being visitors from out of town. As the business population moved house into

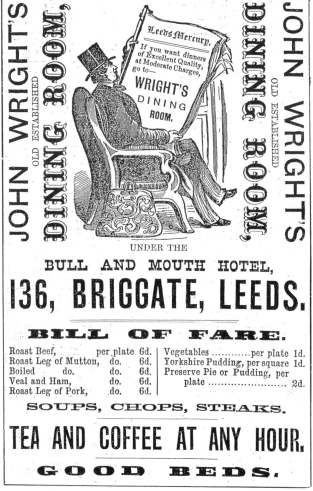

John Wright's dining room, under the Bull and Mouth in Briggate, offered a selection of very good basic meals for people working in the town centre.

the suburbs, it was no longer convenient to travel home and back for dinner, and so the inns and hotels began to provide the classic businessman's lunch in their dining rooms. John Wright's Dining Room at the Bull and Mouth in Briggate offered roast and boiled meats, vegetables, squares of Yorkshire pudding and fruit pie or pudding for "afters", the kind of food which was certainly appreciated by most businessmen in similar dining rooms certainly up to the 1960s. 1880 saw the start of a much-loved Leeds institution, when the old Turk's Head was converted into Whitelock's First City Luncheon Bar, its mirrored signs on Briggate advertising "The Pioneer Luncheon Bar …Tea, Coffee, Wines, Beer and Spirits, …Light

Lunches from 11am …Teas, Suppers" etc. The interior of its long bar and dining room, resplendent with etched mirrors, colourful tiling, polished brass and other period features, still remains in its original condition, and is still renowned for maintaining the best traditions of English pub food. The great haunches of rare-roast beef on their silvered platters, surrounded by bowls of horseradish, mustard and pickles, no longer stand on its bar as formerly, but all its other fare, especially its roast beef and Yorkshire pudding are still greatly enjoyed today.

For those who wanted something rather more spacious and formal, both for business lunches and for dining out in the evenings, and also to cater for the thousands of agents and travellers, etc., who now came to conduct business with Leeds-based companies, there was a great expansion in the hotel sector. By 1880 the Queen's Hotel, the Trevelyan Temperance Hotel (now the Leeds Marriott Hotel), the Griffin, the Guildford, the Victoria, and the Golden Lion, which all continue today, had all been rebuilt to the highest standards. They all offered good dining facilities, probably the finest being those at the Queen's, where the dining room was completely clad in the finest white and gold Burmantofts tiling in 1904. This was both visually attractive and, being totally non-absorbent, was easily cleaned and ensured that the room never held any stale food odours. Complete with its crystal chandeliers, mural paintings, bar, and balcony where musicians could play string instruments to accompany the meals, it was a delightful setting in which to enjoy table d'hôte meals such as the following, dating from a little earlier, 18 May 1895:

Soup:	Clear Oxtail or Thick Asparagus
Fish:	Salmon, Hollandaise Sauce
Joint:	Roast Lamb
Poultry:	Roast Chicken
	Salade
Sweets:	Diplomatic Pudding, Vanilla Ice, Pastry
Dessert	

Comparable meals were served at the other Leeds hotels, this menu coming from the Albion Hotel on 24 June 1899:

Soup:	Juleinne
Fish:	Boiled Turbot & Lobster Sauce
Joints:	Roast Beef, Boiled Mutton
Poultry:	Roast Chicken
Sweets:	Jelly, Blancmange, Stewed Fruits
Dessert	

Perhaps the finest food in Leeds was to be found in the restaurants. In 1880 there were very few independent restaurants in the centre, but by 1890 there were over a dozen, such as the Athenaeum, the Clarence, the Albert, the Grand, the Monaco, the Silver Grid, the St James', Brayshay's, and, best of all Adolph Powolny's at 4 & 5 Bond Street. Established as Artistic Confectioners in 1862, Powolny's maintained the highest standards, always keeping live turtles in stock for making real turtle soup, and holding cellars full of the most excellent wines.[12] They were responsible for catering for many of the royal visits and other civic ceremonies in Leeds, at which they served dinners and suppers quite equal to any which could have been provided by the very best London companies.

Resplendent in its white and gold Burmantofts faience tile-clad walls, its painted murals, potted palms and well-stocked bar, the Queen's Hotel offered probably the best hotel dining facilities in early Edwardian Leeds. *(Leeds Library & Information Services).*

Imagine sitting down to the following luncheon Adolph Powolny cooked for the Shah of Persia and civic guests in the Central Court of the Art Gallery on 26 July 1889:

Hot

	Turtle Soup, Mulligatawny Soup
Milk Punch	Salmon in Curry, Fillets of Soles, Normande
	Lamb Cutlets
Hock-Niersteiner	Quenelles of Foies-gras

Cold

Claret-St Julien	Salmon, Fillets of Soles, Aspic
Champagne:	Galantine of Chicken, Sirloin of Beef
Jules Mumm, 1884	Quarter of Lamb, Roast Chickens
Pommery & Grenno	Yorkshire Ham
	Leveret Pie, Roast Pigeons, Truffled Quails
	Norwegian Salad
Liqueurs:	German Torte, Champagne Jelly
Maraschino	Vanilla Cream, Ice Pudding
Chartreuse	
Cognac	Fruit

Notes:
1. P. Brears, *The Kitchen Catalogue,* York (1979)no.22
2. Leeds Local History Library, Sales Catalogues
3. F. R. Spark, *Memories of my Life,*Leeds (n.d.)144-8 & J. Mayhall, *Annals of Yorkshire,* (1878)II 432
4. R .de V. Renwick, *English Folk Poetry*, Pennsylvania (1980)135-6
5. Leeds Local History Library, Sales Catalogues
6. *ibid.,* "Royal Visits to Leeds 1858-1868",33
7. C. Gilbert, *Furniture at Temple Newsam House and Lotherton Hall,* Leeds (1978)283-7
8. Castle Museum, York, MS recipe book of Ellen Bulmer of St Mark's Villa, Leeds, 1878
9. T. W. Reid, *Memoir of Kohn Deakin Heaton, M.D.,* (1883)101-4
10. E. Driver, *A Bibliography of Cookery Books Published in Britain 1875-1914,* (1989)387
11. *Yorkshire Evening Post,4/4/1913 & 23/10/1920*

GREAT BANQUETS

THERE are few more pleasurable and memorable ways in which to celebrate any special event, than to hold a banquet. It is the ideal way in which to promote good fellowship, extend hospitality, and provide the perfect setting for expressing thanks and appreciation to all concerned. In Victorian Leeds some of the great banquets were truly spectacular, and demonstrate a degree of sheer wealth, taste, culinary skill and formidable gastric fortitude which is quite amazing by any modern standards.

Leeds folk have always enjoyed the opportunity of partaking large formal meals even if, for most working people, these were very infrequent affairs. To celebrate some great national event, however, their employers sometimes provided them with a feast. To mark the Golden Jubilee of George III on 25 October 1809, Rothwell celebrated with a roasted ox and quantities of fine ale largely provided by Thomas, William and James Fenton, the great "coal-kings of Yorkshire".[1]

In honour of his majesty, they roasted a fat beast,
And gave away most freely, that all should have a taste …

The coals that made the fire to roast this ox
Was drawn by sixteen stallions, and they were jovial bucks,
The gentleman he drove them with a stick and a bladder,
And he took great delight in keeping them together.

Near unto the churchyard a public house is there
At which he stopped his team, and watered them with beer,
There was a great report we should be short of ale,
But if there had been more, our barrels would not fail.

A guinea there was given by a noble gentleman,
For a posset and a dance, disprove it if you can:
On Tuesday afternoon the women merry were
In drinking of this posset, and plenty of good cheer.

So here's a health unto his majesty, likewise to Mr Pitt,
Likewise to Dr Willis, we've not forgot him yet:
Here's a health to these miners, they are men of great
     renown,
Likewise to all true subjects of famous Rothwell town.

To celebrate the prospect of peace, and the predicted boom in trade which would follow the end of the Napoleonic wars, Messrs Gott and Wormald of the Bean Ing woollen mills on Wellington Street arranged a very similar event in April 1814. Their employees "paraded the streets with a fleece and other emblems of their manufacture, after regaling plentifully on roast beef and ale, by the liberality of those gentlemen, who caused an ox to be roasted whole …"[2] The actual end of the wars following Napoleon's defeat at Waterloo in 1815, saw further oxen being roasted, the next celebration being the coronation of George IV on 19 July 1821. To mark this event James Hargreaves of the Mill-Garth woollen mills provided a dinner for all his employees, the details being recorded by

John Yewdall, the leading working-class poet of Georgian Leeds:[3]

The yard of Mill-Garth Mills, near the present Police building, was the scene of a dinner to celebrate George IV's birthday on 19 July 1821. Here 200 employees sat down to roast beef and plum pudding, with appropriate quantities of good beer.

His servants to treat, with plenty of meat,
And cheer up their hearts for a while:
The scene was the yard, where duly prepared,
The following sight made 'em smile:

A table was made, upon which were laid,
Twenty four plum puddings compact:
Roast beef and good beer, that old English cheer,
Were plac'd in their order exact.

Two hundred or more, of rich and of poor,
Were seated down in one ring:
When silence profound, was kept all around,
While the band played "God Save the King".
After dinner
Then each took his way, well pleased with the day,
To his well-beloved offspring and dame:
A gill of good beer, next morn, fine and clear,
Each servant received, when he came.

As this quote confirms, banqueting was seen as an entirely masculine activity, women only being admitted as spectators, even at the great late Victorian dinners.

The merchants also used banqueting as a means of making their business meetings much more effective and satisfying. When the trustees of the White Cloth Hall came to check the accounts at their annual meeting, they were not dismayed to find that quite threequarters of their expenditure was concerned with the good things they themselves had consumed. Bottles of wine, currant bread, buns, cheese, and dinners at the Black Bull and White Swan frequently appear in the early 19th century, but in 1810 they held a banquet of very substantial quality, at which they ate, among other items:[4]

	£	s	d
26lb 12oz Beef @ 11d per lb	1	4	6
12lb of Mutton @ 8½d		8	6
6lb 8oz of Veal		3	9½
7lb of Hang [salt] Beef at 1s		7	
6 Pigons		3	
5 Fowls		8	
1lb of Beef			8
15lb of Ham		17	6
4 Rowls of Butter @ 1s 7d		6	4
24 Duck eggs		4	
2lb of Beef Sewett		1	6
Wheat Flower		1	6
Bread		10	
Sparrowgrass and Cabbage		2	1
Cucumber			10
Disart Oranges and Nuts		11	8
Wine, Brandy, Rum and Porter	2	14	9

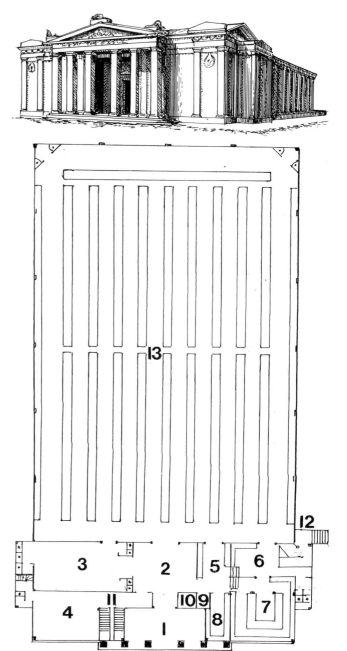

Later accounts show that there was no abatement of these luxuries, details of lamb, peas, gooseberry puddings, salmon, cucumber, gin, brandy, soda water, cigars, etc., all making regular appearances. These dinners appear quite abstemious and plain affairs, however, when compared to the great political banquets mounted first by the Conservative party, and then by the Liberals.

Early in the reign of Queen Victoria, when both parties were battling for control of the newly-reformed borough council, the Conservatives obtained a great boost when Sir Francis Burdett, a leading Liberal politician, switched his allegiance to the Tories. Using the third anniversary of the Leeds Operatives Conservative Society as an excuse, the local party organised a Grand Conservative Festival. For this purpose R. D. Chantrell, the town's leading architect, designed a magnificent pavilion in Park Row, its chaste Grecian exterior having a large portico enriched with the royal arms. Passing through a porch and a hall, flanked by cloakrooms, bars and service rooms, guests entered a magnificent saloon. Measuring 120 by 80ft, it had white calico walls, deep crimson pillars, festoons and drapery by Mr Constantine the upholsterer, and large circular chandeliers illuminated by gas, the whole design resembling the finest interiors of Pompeii and Herculaneum. At 5.15pm on Monday, 16 April 1838, the guests began to arrive, and shortly before 7pm 1,150 gentlemen sat down to their sumptuous dinner, made by Mr Ash of the Angel Hotel, while 500 of their ladies observed the proceedings from their 5s (25p) and half-crown (12.5p) seats in the galleries. After the dinner, its long series of speeches and toasts, and entertainment by Leeds Old Band and Glee Singers, the last guests departed at 2am.[5]

By the time the guests arrived for the Grand Ball at 7pm on the following Friday evening, the entire appearance of the saloon had been changed, the tables being cleared away, and in their place the bare straw-coloured floor decorated with coloured chalk patterns executed to Chantrell's designs by John Wood. There were 12 major compartments for quadrilles, some featuring the rose, thistle, leek and shamrock of the United Kingdom, others with the Star of Brunswick, etc., all brilliantly executed. Along the whole 120ft north wall "ran confectioner's tables, which were very tastefully decorated and amply stored with the choicest viands, liqueurs, fruits, etc., by Mr Bullivant of Boar Lane, offering ample refreshment between the dances accompanied by Mr Horobin's Quadrille Band, and the Band of

The Conservative Pavilion on Park Row in 1838. This massive hall was built for just a single dinner and a ball, and was then demolished, Designed by R. D. Chantrell, it included:

1. **Porch**
2. **Hall**
3. **Gentlemen's Waiting Room**
4. **Ladies' Cloak Room**
5. **Bar**
6. **Waiter's Room**
7. **Pantries**
8. **Wine Cellar**
9. **Spirit Bar**
10. **Check-keeper's Box**
11. **Stairs to Five Shilling Gallery**
12. **Stairs to Half-crown Gallery**
13. **The Saloon, filled with tables and chairs**

the 11th Hussars." After the last of the six or seven hundred guests left at 4am, the whole building was dismantled, and its site cleared. This whole exercise had been designed to demonstrate the wealth, power and elegant taste of the Leeds Conservatives, but the Liberals decided not to be impressed, their newspaper, the *Leeds Mercury* christening the whole event

The newly-built Town Hall afforded magnificent dining facilities, either for hundreds in the Victoria Hall, or for more select groups in the suite of Mayor's Rooms. To serve both there were large kitchens in the basement. This engraving shows the banquet held on 27 May 1859, to celebrate George Skirrow Beecoft's re-election as MP for the borough. *(Leeds Library & Information Services)*.

"The Revel of the Rats" in honour of Sir Francis' desertion of their party. To them, the pavilion was a great "triumph of paint and calico, of leather and prunella over the nakedness of deal boards" and merely the "unrivalled, nay unequalled Leeds Rat Trap"!

The Conservatives organised a further banquet in the newly-built Town Hall on 27 May 1859 to celebrate the return of George Skirrow Beecroft into his second term as MP for Leeds. Seven hundred guests, seated at long tables according to their electoral wards, were entertained by Tidswell's Band of Music as they dined on fare provided by Mr Ash of the Wheatsheaf in Upper Headrow. The ladies filled the balcony and the orchestra seats to hear the speeches afterwards.[6] It must have been a very jolly affair, for at the end of the evening G. S. Beecoft's nephews had to be carried into their carriage, and completed the journey back to their home in Kirkstall with their legs dangling out of the windows.

It took the Liberals over 40 years to mount anything to equal the Conservative Festival, but when they did so, they did it with real style. At the 1880 election, after six years of Disraeli's Conservative government, William Gladstone swept back into power with a great Liberal victory, and as MP for both Leeds and Midlothian. In October 1881, Gladstone, now Prime Minister, came on a two-day visit to Leeds to thank his supporters for their unwavering assistance. Here he was feted with an enthusiasm which outshone even that extended to royalty. By Friday, 7 October, most of the preparations were complete. The vast central courtyard of the Coloured Cloth Hall, which occupied the present City Square, General Post Office and Cloth Hall Court sites, had been totally roofed over by the Leeds architect Thomas Ambler to create a gigantic

banqueting hall to seat 1,300 gentlemen, with hundreds of places for the ladies in the huge raised gallery. For decoration, there were numerous flags, swags, wreaths and mottoes, the hall being lit by a combination of roof-lights, gas lights and the new electric lamps. "The effect of the two means of illumination was very brilliant and showed to advantage the decoration of this temporary building" wrote a reporter, even if the electrics failed before the end of the function. The most amazing part of the whole affair, however, was the menu:

Soups:	Clear Game Soup
	Potage Creme d'Orge
Fish:	Filets of Soles à la Tartare
	Mayonnaise of Lobster
	Eels en Bastion
Entree:	Filets de Volaille en chaud froid
	Noix de Veau
	Venison Cutlets à la d'Orsay
	Veal and Ham Pies
Roasts:	Roast Mutton à la Provencale
	Turkeys à la Imperatrice
	Beef à la Mode
	Tongues
	Chickens à la Bechamel
	Roast Beef.
	Hams
	Roast Chickens
Game:	Galantine of Pheasants
	Grouse
	Partridges
	Roast Pheasants
	Game Pies

On 21 October 1881, the Liberals celebrated Mr Gladstone's return both as a local MP and as Prime Minister, by organising a vast banquet for 1,300 people in this specially-built hall constructed within the courtyard of the coloured Cloth Hall. As may be seen, it has both gas and the new electric lighting, the latter failing ignominiously during the evening. *(Leeds Library & Information Services)*.

Dessert: Gelee au Marasquin
           Cremes Bavaroises
           Gateaux d'Artois
           Charlotte Russe au Café
           Tartlettes à la Parisienne
           Puddings aux Fruits

A total of 28 dishes, to be prepared and served quickly and efficiently to 1,300 diners, all by the staff of the Queen's Hotel. Even if the food was simple, it would present a considerable challenge, but this was food of the greatest quality and complexity. The menu appears to have been largely based on Joules Gouffe's *Le Livre de Cuisine* published in Paris in 1867, and, having been translated into English by his brother Alphonse, head pastrycook to Queen Victoria, published in London in 1869 as *The Royal Cookery Book*. Even in the gastronomic circles of Paris, these recipes were regarded as outstanding examples of garnishing and presentation, and real challenges to any chef. There is no room here to describe all the dishes in detail, but as an example, we can follow the preparation of just one, the *Eels en Bastion*.

First two eels were boned, stuffed with a truffled forcemeat of fat bacon and tongue, rolled in a napkin, trussed, simmered in a savoury stock, cooled, unwrapped, cut in four-inch lengths, and coated in clear fish glaze. A large mound of cooked rice was then formed on a dish and covered with butter flavoured with anchovies, egg yolks, oil and vinegar, and stained bright green with pounded gherkins, anchovies, chervil, tarragon, burnet, chives and cress. This formed the mount on which the castle of

eels would now be built. One piece of eel was then stood vertically on top of the mound, and surrounded by four other pieces to form flanking towers. Sheets of chilled green butter were next formed into a continuous floor over the eels, walls between the towers, and mouldings around their tops and bases. A further section of eel was then placed on top of the others, similarly decorated, and then all the towers were topped by "battlements" cut from poached fillets of sole. Finally "firing loops" cut from boiled egg-white were added to each tower, and the surrounding "moat" filled with a glittering layer of chopped aspic jelly. This spectacular dish would serve six people, and was one of three dishes served in the fish course, which means that the chefs at the Queen's Hotel would have to make around 72 of these spectacular dishes, in addition to all the other demands being made on their overstretched resources.

Although the participants all enjoyed their dinners, dining to the music of the Grenadier Guards, Mr Gladstone decided not to arrive until it was time for the speeches, when, after the loyal toasts to the Queen, The Army, the Navy, and the health of the Prime Minister, etc., he delivered one of his most significant speeches on the Irish Question. At ten o'clock, he finally departed by coach to the house of James Kitson, now the Leeds Girl's High School on Headingley Lane, the entire route being illuminated by between two and three thousand people bearing flaming torches, and accompanied by bands of music.

As well as political banquets, others were organised to welcome important visitors to the town. In August 1856 a major banquet was held in honour of the Earl of Cardigan, the

Charlotte Russe au Café

Filets de Volaille en chaud froid

Eels en Bastion

The food prepared for the Gladstone banquet was all of the most demanding international standard, as may be seen from these drawings of a selection of the dishes.

popular leader of the Charge of the Light Brigade at Balaclava, and owner of much of Headingley and Kirkstall. The organising committee employed Mr Jackson of Wellington Street to decorate the hall of the Leeds Stock Exchange, on the corner of Albion Street and Albion Place, with a colourful mass of flags, swags, mottoes, portraits and allegorical figures. Mr Wilks of the White Horse Hotel on Boar Lane then set out a fine luncheon for the gentlemen guests, the ladies, as usual, being confined to the gallery. As the Earl took his seat at 1pm, Tidswell's Railway Foundry Band struck up *The Roast Beef of Old England* from the balcony outside, and played throughout the meal. The proceedings concluded at 4.20pm, after numerous speeches, toasts, and the presentation of a fine specially commissioned sword to the Earl, on behalf of the people of Yorkshire.

Two years later, Queen Victoria and Prince Albert were given lunch before their departure after opening the Town Hall, the Mayor then giving a banquet for 400 guests, the catering being provided by the Leeds confectioner, Mr Godfrey Wood.

Further royal visits brought more banquets, but rather than reviewing them all, it is perhaps best to look at one in some detail. In 1862-8 the new Leeds General Infirmary had been built to the designs of Sir George Gilbert Scott, with advice from Florence Nightingale, as one of the finest hospitals in Europe. It had spacious, well-ventilated wards, and a glass-roofed winter garden in which patients could sit among exotic plants. For its opening, before any patients were admitted, the whole huge building was used as a gigantic temporary art gallery for a National Exhibition of Works of Art, showing

paintings and antiquities loaned by numerous private and public owners. The opening was performed at midday on 19 May 1868, by HRH The Prince of Wales, on behalf of Queen Victoria. After the Hallelujah Chorus had been performed, the Prince, accompanied by 50 guests, including over a dozen peers, the Lord Mayor of London, the Mayor of Leeds, and the Bishop of Ripon, took luncheon in the refreshment room, this being provided by Messrs Spiers and Pond:

Pottage:	Pottage printanier Royal
Hors d'oeuvres:	Pâté de Foies Gras aux Truffles
	Anchois en Salade
Entrees:	Balotines de Volaile à la Princesse
	Petits Pates à la Reine
	Cotelettes d'Agneau aux Concombres
	Ris de Veau Pique au Petit Pois
Releves:	Les Galantines de Dinde aux truffes
	Langues de Boeuf
	Jambon en Aspic
	Galantines de Poulardes Mazaran
	Chapons à la Bechamelle
	Chapons Rotis
	Mayonnaise de Homard à la Gelee
	Salade de Volaille
	Terrine de Vollaile aux Foies Gras
	Cailles à la Royale aux truffes
	Crevettes de Dieppe
	Asperges à la Sauce Venetienne
	Chouxfleurs au Gratin
Entremets:	Poudings de Savois
	Gelee de Dansic au Cerises
	Creme d'Orange
	Cremes à la Vanilla
	Gateaux de Genoise aux Conserves
	Gelees claires au Marasquin
	Poudings Glaces à la Nesselrode
	Dessert de Saison

This may be translated as:

Soups:	Clear spring vegetable soup with cubes of savoury custard
Hors d'oeuvres:	Truffled goose-liver pâté
	Anchovy Salad
Entrees:	Chicken legs stuffed with chicken forcemeat, braised in white wine, chopped onions, garlic, tomatoes, etc., garnished with French beans and saute potatoes
	Small tarts of rich chicken puree
	Lamb cutlets with cucumbers
	Calf sweetbreads with green peas
Releves:	Turkey formed into a roll, poached, with truffles
	Ox tongue
	Ham in aspic jelly
	Fat hen formed into a roll, poached, garnished with artichokes, vegetables, veal dumplings, etc.
	Capon with white sauce
	Roast Capon
	Lobster mayonnaise with aspic
	Poultry sala
	Terrine of poultry with goose-liver pâté
	Quail garnished with both chicken and veal

Until the Town Hall was opened in 1858, the best venue for great banquets was the hall of the Leeds Stock Exchange in Albion Street. Here it is in August 1856, when the people of Yorkshire presented a sword to the Earl of Cardigan, leader of the Charge of the Light Brigade, and the owner of most of Headingley and Kirkstall.

dumplings, slices of goose-liver, mushrooms, cock's combs and truffles

Prawns, with shrimps, mussels and white-wine sauce

Asparagus with white wine sauce and green herb butter

Cauliflowers, boiled, covered in Mornay sauce and grated cheese, finished in the oven

Entremets: Puddings of Savoy sponge?

Jelly of Dansic gold-leaf liqueur and cherries

Orange cream

Vanilla cream

Genoese pastries with fruit conserves

Maraschino liqueur jelly

Ice cream pudding of vanilla filled with Chantilly cream and crushed glace chestnuts

Dessert: Fruits in season

With all the high quality of garnishing and culinary art available at this time, this must have been one of the most sparkling, almost jewel-like of meals, every item decorated to the most ornate, colourful and sparkling stylish perfection. This was only part-way through the day's events, however, for Victorian society demonstrated great stamina on such occasions.

At 10pm the same day, the guests began to assemble for the ball in the Town Hall, the Prince arriving at midnight to open the dancing by partnering the Lady Mayoress in a quadrille. In the small hours the thousand guests were "sumptuously regaled" in the supper rooms, but for the 50 special guests, a separate table had been prepared for them in the Mayor's

apartments. Messrs Hunt & Roshell of Bond Street provided all the silverware, and Phillips & Pearce also of Bond Street all the glassware, to ensure that everything was of the very best. As for the supper itself, it was cooked by A. Lecour of 7, Oak Terrace, Battersea:

Potages:	Consommé Victoria
	Creme liee à la Cobourg
Entrees:	Supreme de Volaille à la Richelieu
	Cotelettes d'Agneau Alexandra
	Cailles de Vigne bardees
	Poularde piquee
	Mayonnaise de Homard en Belle Vue
	Truit du Loch Tay au bleu
	Terrine de Foies Gras truffes
	Galantine sur sogne historiees
	Jambon de Westphalie
Suplement:	Buisson d'Oeufs de Pluviers à la gelee
	Gradius de Crevettes
Entremets:	Gelee de Champagne aux frits
	Mousse à la Taglioni
	Baba à la Polonaise
	Croquant à la Russe
	Patisserie variee
Dessert.	

This may be translated as:

Soups:	Clear beef or chicken soup, with strips of chicken, truffles, peas, chervil and small chicken dumplings
	Thick Coburg soup
Entrees:	Chicken breasts, dipped in egg and bread-

69

crumbs, fried in butter, decorated with slices of glazed truffles, served with green herb butter

Lamb cutlets probably with truffle slices, Mornay sauce and asparagus tips

Quail wrapped in vine leaf and bacon, roast, and probably served with madeira and veal gravy, garnished with peeled seeded grapes

Fat hen

Cold Dishes: Lobster mayonnaise dressed and garnished in sumptuous style

Loch Tay trout, poached, served with melted butter, grated horseradish and potatoes

Pate of goose-liver with truffles

Westphalia ham

Plover's eggs

Prawns

Entremets: Champagne jelly with poached fruits

Mousse

Yeast-raised sponge cake soaked with liqueur syrup

A tall column of crisp almond biscuits stuck together with caramel

Pastries

Dessert: Fresh fruits

Menus for meals served at other royal visits to Leeds, such as the luncheon given to the Duke and Duchess of York at Temple Newsam on 5 October 1894, when they came to open the Leeds Medical School, show that this quality of entertainment was quite usual at this level of society.

Major dinners were also given to the Judges of Assize when they came to hold their courts in the Town Hall, for Leeds had become Assize town for the whole of the West Riding in 1864. In the 1890s, these followed a fairly standard pattern, varied by the seasonal availability of the raw ingredients, oysters and game being more usual in winter, and hors d'oeuvres in summer, for example. These dinners were served a la Russe, each dish being handed to the individual guests by the waiters, and now included alcoholic sorbets between the roasts and the poultry, etc., as a means of refreshing the palate halfway through the meal. The following menu was prepared by Adolph Powolny for the dinner given by the Mayor, Alderman Ward, to Lord Chief Justice Lord Coleridge and the Hon. Sir Gainsford Bruce at the opening of the Summer Assize, 31 July 1893:

	Hors d'oeuvres
Soups:	Tortue Claire
	Bisque d'Ecrevisses
Poissons:	Turbot, Hollandaise
	Whitebait a la Diable
Entrees:	Cotelettes a la Financier
	Pigeons aux petit pois
	Ris de Veau, Godard
Releve:	Filet de Boeuf a la Bearnaise
Sorbet:	Sorbet Marasquin
Rot:	Poulet frit a la Tartare
	Chevreuil Bohemienne
	Aloyau Roti
	Jambon d'York
Entremets:	Ortolans rotis
	Homard a la Russe
	Omelette aux Framboises
	Charlotte Parisienne
	Pouding Glace Nesselrode
Dessert	Dessert

The other regular feature of late Victorian and Edwardian civic life was the Mayor's Dinner, usually held in the week before Christmas for members of the corporation and guests such as the magistrates, neighbouring mayors, and senior officers such as the Town Clerk and the Borough Engineer. They were fine high-class Christmas Dinners of some seven to nine courses and included real turtle soup, a fine fish course, a variety of entrees, turkey, York ham and similar substantial joints, pheasant and lobster salads, plum pudding, mince pies, ice creams and a dessert of fresh fruit, followed by various toasts. Here is a typical Mayor's Dinner prepared for the Mayor, John Ward, and the corporation, on 19 December 1892:

	Oysters	
Soup:	Turtle Soup	
	Pheasant Soup	
Fish:	Salmon, Sauce Hollandaise	
	Fillets of Soles	
Entrees:	Pigeon Cutlets	Mushrooms
	Mutton Cutlets	Beans
	Snipe on Toast	Asparagus Points
Removes:	Roast Turkey	
	Ox Tongue	
	Sirloin of Beef	
	Yorkshire Ham & Spinach	
Game:	Pheasants	
	Lobster Salad	
Sweets:	Plum Pudding	
	Mince Pies	
	Lemon Jelly	
	Vanilla Cream	
	Strawberry Ice	
Dessert:	Dessert of Fresh Fruit	

Civic hospitality on this scale continued throughout the Edwardian period, and into the inter-war years, but since that time great dinners have fallen out of fashion. This is partly due to economic reasons, partly to social reasons, and partly because most people today would feel physically uncomfortable after eating their way through numerous consecutive courses of rich food.

However, as far as the individual dishes are concerned, these are just as enjoyable today as they were in the past. This was amply proved in 1993, when the Lord Mayor, Cllr Keith Loudon, conceived the idea of bringing together the city's major hotels and charities, and organising a series of fund-raising charity dinners, each based on an historic Leeds menu. At the Leeds Fair Dinner in the Town Hall, for example, everyone enjoyed the roast beef, plumb pudding, Fair cakes and parkin pigs, for example, along with the wrestling matches, community singing, and Simon Lindley's performance of *Leeds Old Fair*. At the Queen's Hotel, meanwhile, guests were very appreciative of the gastronomic delights of the Gladstone Banquet faithfully recreated by its chef and his staff, and also of the Gladstone Speech given by Lord Merlyn Rees. In this way hundreds of people learned something of the history of their city in the most enjoyable way possible, for, like all good meals, these historic Leeds dinners satisfied all the participant's senses of sight, smell, touch, taste and hearing.

Notes:

1. J. Batty, *The History of Rothwell,* Rothwell (1877) 65
2. *Leeds Mercury,* 13/4/1814
3. J. Yewdall, *The Toll Bar,* (1827) 55
4. "The Leeds White Cloth Hall", *Thoresby Society,* Leeds (19..) 152-3
5. *The Leeds Mercury,* 28/5/1859
6. *ibid.,* 2/9/1856

INDEX